CITYSCAPES AND CAPITAL

CITYSCAPES AND CAPITAL

THE POLITICS OF URBAN DEVELOPMENT

Michael A. Pagano

and Ann O'M. Bowman

THE JOHNS HOPKINS UNIVERSITY PRESS

Baltimore and London

© 1995, 1997 The Johns Hopkins University Press
All rights reserved. Published 1995
Printed in the United States of America on acid-free paper

Johns Hopkins Paperbacks edition, 1997
06 05 04 03 02 01 00 99 98 97   5 4 3 2 1

The Johns Hopkins University Press
2715 North Charles Street
Baltimore, Maryland 21218-4319
The Johns Hopkins Press Ltd., London

Library of Congress Cataloging-in-Publication Data will be
found at the end of this book.
A catalog record for this book is available from the British
Library.

ISBN 0-8018-5034-7
ISBN 0-8018-5767-8 (pbk.)

For Deborah, Gina, and Andrea—M.A.P.

For Carson—A.O'M.B.

CONTENTS

List of Figures   ix

List of Tables   x

Preface to the Paperback Edition   xi

Preface and Acknowledgments   xiii

1. Politics Matters   1
    The Argument   2
    The Methods   4
    The Cities   9

2. Public Capital, Systems of Cities, and Perceptual Orbits   20
    Mobilizing Public Capital   21
    Central-Place Theory: The Conventional Wisdom   29
    Politics and the Systems of Cities   33
    Perceptual Orbits   37
    Concluding Observations   43

3. Aspirations, Visions, and Images   44
    The Concept of Image   44
    Images and Economic Development   48
    Image Creation   50
    The Study Cities and Their Images   51
    Concluding Observations   67

4. Cities and Economic Development   68
    Market Failure   69
    Government Failure   72
    Government Market Failure: Failure of a Third Kind   76
    Development Tools   84
    Concluding Observations   91

5. Measuring Successful Development   92
    Market Failure and Government Success   94
    Redefining Success and Failure   95
    Development Project Findings   97
    Concluding Observations   104

6. Urban Outcomes   106
    Three Interrelated Development Outcomes   106
    Project Outcomes   111
    Concluding Observations   134

7. On Politics, Markets, and Images   137
    Dynamic Visions and Aspirations   138
    Development Projects: Tentative Lessons   140
    A City's Limits   142

Appendixes   143
    A. City Population and Land Area   144
    B. The Development Tools Used by the Study Cities   147

Notes   163

Index   179

FIGURES

1.1   The Location of the Study Cities   7

2.1   The Tax-Services Equilibrium Model   27

2.2   The Economic Ranges of the Study Cities   32

2.3   The Perceptual Orbits of Boise and Orlando   38

3.1   Huntsville Logo Inspired by the Space Industry   55

6.1   Duluth's Storefront Renovation   112

6.2   Lowell's Wannalancit Mills Office and Technology Center   114

6.3   Springfield's City Market and Hotel Project   115

6.4   Boise's Towne Square Mall   117

6.5   Duluth's Fond-du-Luth Casino   119

6.6   Lowell's Eastern Canal Park (Jack Kerouac Commemorative Park)   121

6.7   Boise's Downtown before Development   122

6.8   Boise's Downtown after Development   122

6.9   Independence's Independence Square   125

6.10 Evansville's Walnut Centre Area before Development   127

6.11 Evansville's Walnut Centre Area after Development   127

6.12 Lowell's Hilton Hotel   130

6.13 Beaumont's Texas Energy Museum   132

6.14 Santa Barbara's La Colina Housing Project   133

TABLES

4.1 Sources of City Revenue, 1977–1991   78

4.2 Investment in Springfield's City Market and Hotel   81

4.3 Level of Financial Risk, Development Incentive Packages
of the Study Cities   86

4.4 Level of Financial Risk, Routine Incentive Packages
of the Study Cities   88

5.1 Six Characteristics of Development Tools and Prediction
of Project Success   99

5.2 Six Characteristics of Development Tools and Prediction of
Revenue Generation   102

6.1 Duluth's Central Business District: Property Value,
Property Tax, and Sales Tax, 1978–1988   113

6.2 Value of Building Permits for Evansville's Walnut Centre
Area   128

6.3 Intents and Outcomes of the 12 Development Projects   135

PREFACE TO

THE PAPERBACK EDITION

AMERICAN CITIES CONTINUE to mold themselves into the kinds of communities that will flourish in the twenty first century. Central to the effort, as we argue in this book, is the vision of local leaders and their willingness to use public capital to pursue that vision. Since the book's publication, that realization has spread beyond the scholarly world to the popular press. For example, in the issue appearing November 1, 1996, *Newsweek* ran an article called "City Slickers." The story featured mayors with high aspirations for their communities—those who were taking bold stands, initiating new programs, and in the process, transforming their cities. Detroit's mayor is credited with putting together deals to turn the former General Motors headquarters into a new city hall and to construct new stadiums for the city's professional baseball and football teams. As manufacturing dried up in downtown Louisville, the city government laid the groundwork to convert the area into a vibrant cultural center. For many cities, however, the aspiration is not for glittering new facilities or a reinvented city; instead, the effort is directed at maintaining the community and avoiding the loss of the city's natural attributes. For example, the mayor of San Jose promoted the "Greenline Initiative," which would dramatically slow the development of nearly 100,000 acres of hills, farms, and wetlands around the city. These cases have a common characteristic: local leaders with vision—albeit not the same vision—and a commitment to translating this vision into reality.

Is this activity about jobs, as many economists would have us believe? Is employment the central goal in a city's development program? We find that jobs are a means to an end, and the end is to ensure an adequate supply of revenue for the purpose of maintaining an acceptable level of services. Mayors and other city politicians certainly avail themselves of any ribbon-cutting ceremony for development projects that promise jobs; the publicity is good. But city politicians taking advantage of photo opportunities does not mean that the purpose of city government intervention in the market is jobs-driven. Rather, the impetus behind mobilizing public capital and investing city resources in development comes not from a downturn in jobs, but from a downturn in revenue—which may or may not be directly linked to jobs, depending in large part on the tax structure of the city—or a decline in acceptable service levels. Property tax revenue may be affected by job opportunities, and so might income and sales tax revenues. But the revenue needs and service-delivery demands on a heavy-manufacturing city with access solely to the property tax are quite different from those for a retirement community relying solely on a sales tax. In both cities, a different mix of services is provided, and the trigger to provide economic development programs is linked to the broader concern about adequate revenues, not about an optimal level of jobs.

Adequate revenues support an acceptable level of services. And it is the various definitions of *adequate* and *acceptable* that aid our understanding, in part, of the "politics matters" statement in our study. Although our research design did not lead us to examine the personalities of elected and appointed officials, it was evident that politics had shaped the kinds of projects that were sponsored by a city. It is the mental image of a cityscape that drives the selection of development tools, the mobilization and allocation of city resources, and the aggressiveness of city leaders in pursuing their vision. Politics also matters in framing a future cityscape. City leaders may decide to try to propel their community to a higher plane in their city's relevant orbit of cities, or they may be content with the status quo.

The phenomenon of vision creation and image development is interesting and important. Indeed, this vision is not static; rather, it changes as a city's leadership changes. (See Harold Wolman, John Strate, and Alan Melchior, "Does Changing Mayors Matter?" *Journal of Politics* 58 [Feb. 1996]: 201–23.) We hope that other researchers will build on our work by investigating how visions are formed, which groups are instrumental in selling the dominant vision to city leaders, and how power ebbs and flows across major interests in a city.

PREFACE AND
ACKNOWLEDGMENTS

IMAGINE TWO COMMUNITIES in the Rocky Mountain region in the late 1860s. One is located along the transcontinental railroad, the other is 100 miles to the south. Which community would come to dominate the region by the turn of the century? Counterintuitively, the latter community did. There, aggressive entrepreneurs and community leaders orchestrated the completion of a spur linking the town to the railroad and then commenced a promotional campaign on the community's behalf. Over time, that town—Denver—flourished, while the other—Cheyenne—did not. "Left to 'chance,' Denver might have died on the vine."[1] And that is just the point: Denver leaders did not rely on chance. Instead they mobilized public and private resources to pursue their vision: Denver as a major city.

The Denver case is illustrative of our theme. We argue in this book that the critical elements in transforming a community into the cityscape of tomorrow are the vision of its leaders, their commitment to pursue the vision, and their capacity to mobilize public capital for the attainment of that vision. Important too are the strengths, diversity, and resilience of the underlying local economy.

The idea for this book grew out of research we were conducting in the mid-1980s on the development process. We became intrigued with the debate among local officials and scholars about whether development projects mattered or whether development is just another example of follow the leader—if one city does it, others must follow. We found little to help us understand how public capital is mobilized, what outcomes a city expects from any development project, and whether and to what extent these expectations bear fruit. Moreover, we were interested in understanding why one city chooses to mobilize public capital and another refrains, especially when both cities might be expected to respond to a development imperative. Although we always sensed that politics plays a large part in development, we were interested in understanding better how politics matters in city development projects. The watershed event in the evolution of our thinking occurred when a participant at a conference announced in no uncertain terms that "politics was the error term," or residual, in the development calculus. The challenge, then, was to demonstrate that politics does matter; to that end, we spent the next several years collecting data from forty development projects located in ten medium-sized American cities, interviewing city leaders, researching, writing, refining, and replaying our ideas and concepts.

In chapter 1, we argue that the envisioned city of tomorrow is not static; it evolves in response to shifting economies and political coalitions. With the defeat of political coalitions come new visions and images of the city. A city's underlying economy also influences the image and perceptions of city leaders, and these in turn affect the city's economic development function. The bankruptcy of a large manufacturer, the shift of retail sales from old downtown department stores to suburban malls, the realignment of the domestic economy from an industrial to a service base affect not only the tax-to-service balance but also city leaders' perceptions of the city's relevant economic orbit.

In chapter 2, we develop the theory of urban development intervention (public capital mobilization) as a response to a fiscal trigger or to an aspiration of the city's potential. City leaders' perceptions of their city's place within a system of cities and of its systemic competition may be more real than any empirically derived city hierarchy based on spatially determined market areas. Cities are differentially poised to respond to the forces of deindustrialization, reindustrialization, and the new global economy. In life-cycle terminology, older cities may find rejuvenation difficult and reincarnation impossible. They may not have the capacity to spawn new industries, that is, to generate new product cycles.[2] Newer cities, on the other hand, may discover that their relative youth and their distance from older cities are assets. Whatever the city's age, the effort to find a niche—a place where the community fits—is driven by the goals and decisions of city leaders. This niche-seeking is closely linked to what we call perceptual orbits.

We then proceed, in chapter 3, to explore more fully the salience of vision as a key concept in a city's decision to promote economic development projects. And vision is tied to the city's image. For example, for the city of Atlanta, being chosen to host the Summer Olympics was a sign that the city was truly world class. Yet as the city prepared to host the event, "there was a feeling that the city's image was becoming too diffused. . . . There was no clarity of focus as to who we are or what we want to be."[3] Atlanta is not alone in its attention to image. In chapter 3, the ten site-visit cities offer compelling evidence of the power of image.

Chapter 4 turns the notion of market failure, a common explanation for the mobilization of public capital, on its head. Market failure does not explain city government intervention in subsidizing or spurring private or public/private development, nor does it require or precipitate a government response. Rather, government promotion of economic development is legitimized because the market mechanism has proved incapable of providing the "right kind" of spatial incentive and the "right kind" of local competition in the production of spatially bound goods and services. Macrolevel markets in fact succeed when cities are in decline: they signal a higher return on investment and more efficient production and consumption at another location. But the control and authority of local government systems are confined to a finite space, and that space affects the viability of the polity. Perception of market failure by city officials, then, is tied spatially to the real estate over which they exercise control. Public intervention is an important tool in regaining lost spatial-market shares. In chapter 4, examples from two city development projects demonstrate that intervention frequently takes the form of subsidy and investment.

The question of whether public intervention in the development process is successful or not is explored in chapter 5. In particular, we test the link between a set of policy attributes and project success. Success is defined in two ways: in conventional revenue-generation terms and in terms of whether the project accomplished what city officials intended. Although questions still remain, projects that engender political controversy at the time of their proposal are more likely not to succeed than noncontroversial projects. There is also some evidence that simple, tried-and-true projects are more likely to succeed than complex projects. If we examine projects only on revenue generation, the clearest predictor of success is, not surprisingly, the economic health of the city.

The architects of development projects hope these projects influence the pattern of urban development. Chapter 6 takes up the issue of whether they do. Three general outcomes are possible: one is a change in the vista or the physical appearance of the project area, two is a shift in the class of user of the project area, and three is an increase in private capital investment and property values in the project area. In this chapter we examine such consequences, both intended and unintended, and present photographs of twelve of the projects.

In chapter 7, we return to our central themes and reflect upon the lessons that can be drawn from the study.

Each co-author contributed equally to the book. We owe many people a debt of gratitude for their help. Without the generous financial support of the Lincoln Institute of Land Policy, which underwrote the costs of the ten site visits, and the encouragement of its (then) Director of Research Benjamin Chinitz, we would have been unable to carry this project to fruition. Parts of chapter 2 appeared in *Urban Affairs Quarterly,* March 1992, in an article titled "City Intervention: An Analysis of the Public Capital Mobilization Process." Much of the material in chapter 5 was published in the May 1992 issue of *Economic Development Quarterly,* in an article titled "Attributes of Development Tools: Success and Failure in Local Economic Development." The comments of reviewers and editors of those two journals are hereby acknowledged.

We acknowledge as well the insight of the following people regarding ideas in papers we presented at professional meetings and circulated among colleagues: Benjamin Chinitz, Susan Clarke, Arnold Fleischmann, Bryan Jones, Michael Rich, Mark Schneider, and Clarence Stone. In particular, we express our deep gratitude to Harold Wolman and Dennis Judd, both of whom read and critiqued the entire manuscript.

Thanks are also due the following individuals: Earl Black, Steven De-Lue, Eric Frayer, Dan Gould, Jeff Greene, Blaine Liner, and Dorothy Pierson. We thank Henry Tom, executive editor at Johns Hopkins University Press, for his encouragement and assistance. Diane Hammond, our copy editor, refreshed our tired words and labored sentences.

Of course, none of the above mentioned bears any responsibility for errors of omission or commission—that responsibility, as usual, belongs to my coauthor.

CITYSCAPES AND CAPITAL

I / POLITICS MATTERS

IT IS NO ACCIDENT of history that Boston became the center of the shipping industry, Chicago the railroad center for agricultural trade, and Pittsburgh the center of the iron and steel industry. These, and other mighty cities, possessed both abundant natural resources and transportation links that, together with plentiful labor and capital, conspired to promote these cities' fortunes. Nor was the growth in these and other great cities driven solely by an unfettered marketplace. Deliberate city and state actions made Buffalo a great city through its link with Albany along the state-sponsored Erie Canal and Baltimore a great mercantile center because of state and city financing of water projects and railroads. Even the magnificent public works projects of the expanding urban America of the late 1800s—which continue into the present—reduced both market and transportation costs and the costs of exploiting and processing natural resources and manufacturing goods.

City and state investment in transportation infrastructure is well documented.[1] Not only did cities' investment decisions affect their destinies—as either regional hubs or backwater villages—but entrepreneurs soon realized they could force cities to bid against each other for their services, driving public investment costs so high that cities often lost money on such ventures.[2] Although bankruptcy characterized much of city and state investment in canals and railroads in the nineteenth century, cities did not later eschew internal improvement investments or private sector subsidies or any other development activities. Just as canals and railroads were seen as essential in the earlier years of urbanization and industrialization, now cities underwrite airports, sports stadiums, and convention centers. The landscape may have changed, but the behavior remains remarkably constant.

THE ARGUMENT

As product cycles ebb and flow, population and firms migrate, natural resources peter out, and consumer tastes change, cities either adapt to their changing environments or succumb to the invisible hand of the marketplace. Although we view cities as social organizations that attempt to adapt to their changing environments, we also argue that local officials shape how their cities adapt to change by deciding whether to implement nonmarket, city-sponsored development. From our vantage point, this is why politics matters. Although city-sponsored development might lower business costs and spur economic growth, such development is not automatically employed when the economy of the city changes. Rather, public economic development is the result of a purposive political decision and is undertaken selectively.

What motivates officials to spend public capital to enhance their cities' economic growth? In a classic treatment of urban development policy, Paul Peterson argues that cities are in competition with one another and that the development function is the place where this competition is manifest.[3] We argue that development is only one option cities can pursue and is not an autonomic response to the forces of competition; otherwise, all cities would employ as many resources as possible and this is not the case. Politics matters because those conscious and purposive development actions are choices of city leaders.

Local officials pursue development as a means of reaching an ideal, reflecting an image they hold collectively of what their city ought to be. The cities that their city competes with, then, are important. Does Buffalo compete with neighboring Hamburg, with cross-state power New York City, or with its Great Lakes rival, Cleveland? In what areas does it compete? And what does it want to accomplish? City leaders take actions based on their vision of the collective, a vision rooted in their experiences and informed by their theories of urban development. The success of a development project is defined not only in terms of jobs, income, and resource redistribution but also by whether it helps the city realize the ideal. The success of city-sponsored development is also defined in terms of cash flow to the city's treasury, level of private investment, the image of downtown, and the physical look and emotional feel of the city.

Politics matters. In his treatise on the regime paradigm, Clarence Stone argues that it is important to know the composition of a city's governing coalition and what holds the coalition together.[4] The coalition forges policies that presumably benefit the coalition through the city governance structure. From this perspective, politics matters because whoever sits in the seats of city government and determines political arrangements also determines policies (development and otherwise). Yet these policies are also subject to underlying economic forces and structural conditions (e.g., a city dependent on the property tax will pursue policies that do not jeopardize that revenue source). Although it is assumed that business elites gain something of value through city-sponsored development, regime analysis has thus far not answered the question, Why are development policies pursued? And while certainly someone will gain (often the business community), more important overarching concerns may motivate local officials to promote development. Indeed, our contention is that city leaders pursue economic development in response to changing (often deteriorating) fiscal conditions or to perceptions of the new niche they want their city to occupy and not necessarily in response to the needs of the city's business elite.

The choices city leaders make define whether the city will attempt to influence its environment or adapt to it. Cities do not always pursue economic development because, as we argue below, it is a deliberate activity. If they do, jobs and income are the most frequently mentioned reasons given during the numerous photo opportunities at ribbon-cutting ceremonies, but the more important reasons are improving or stabilizing the city's fiscal position and improving the city's standing in its economic orbit.

To meet these challenges, city leaders rely on a vision of their future cityscape. Their role is to define their vision for the city (whether that is moving up or remaining in the same position in the urban hierarchy), to identify the public economic development tools to accomplish that vision, and to decide the extent of city intervention in the process. City leaders thus take action and mobilize capital based on a vision of what they hope and expect their city to become. Cities search for a niche. Cities reestablish, repackage, even reinvent themselves in an attempt to find their niche.

Our argument, then, is that a city seeks economic development for reasons that include its history, its place in its hierarchy of cities, and its aspirations to change, to become a new city or a renewed city. These reasons are constrained by its economic and fiscal foundations. City leaders share an image of their city's place in its relevant system of cities as well as an image of its possibilities. And leadership makes a difference in defining and pursuing those aspirations.

THE METHODS

Our discussion is bolstered by empirical evidence drawn from analyses of 40 city-supported development projects in 10 medium-sized U.S. cities. We do not use the data to test hypotheses; rather, we rely on them to highlight our global propositions about the mobilization of public capital to influence development.

The Selection of Cities

The cities we chose all had 1980 populations between 70,000 and 150,000, a category we felt would provide a set of candidate cities for which we could sort out and measure fairly precisely the impacts of economic development projects but without the confounding effects of large-scale public or private investment projects.

Sixty-six cities meeting the population criterion had responded in 1987 to a survey on city economic development by Ann O'M. Bowman.[5] She used an index ranging from 0 (meaning that none of the 44 development tools identified in the survey had been used) to 1 (meaning that all of the development tools had been used). The average for the 66 responding cities was .39, indicating that the average city used 39 percent of the 44 development tools. For purposes of grouping cities, those above .39 were considered high-activism cities and those below .39, low-activism cities. From the 66 cities, we eliminated those that had not responded to the 1988 Fiscal Conditions Survey administered by the National League of Cities. The universe of cities from which the 10 cities were chosen, then, totaled 46.

Next, because we posited that one trigger for economic development is a disequilibrium between taxes and city services (see chap. 2), we grouped cities based on the Department of Housing and Urban Development's (HUD) urban development action grant (UDAG) rating system for distressed cities. The 1987 UDAG "large city and urban county universe list" categorized and then ranked jurisdictions based on their level of distress. HUD's distress criteria included population growth, poverty level, amount of pre-1940 housing, income growth, job lag, unemployment rate, and "labor surplus area."[6] Conditions in 729 places were evaluated; 442 were "ranked," that is, they were found to be experiencing some level of distress, thereby qualifying for UDAG funds. Of the cities that we eventually selected for this study, Boise, Santa Barbara, Orlando, Huntsville, and Independence were not ranked, an indication of no distress. Of the remaining five cities, Springfield, Ohio, was ranked 81 (the higher the ranking, the more distressed the city), Duluth was 189, Beaumont was 254, Evansville was 267, and Lowell was 434.

In selecting 10 cities from the pool of 46, our goal was to maximize diversity along the activism and distress dimensions as well as to achieve geographic spread. The selected cities possessed the desired diversity, as shown in the list below:

- High activism (>.39), low distress (365–729)

Arvada, .42	*Lowell, .50 (434)*
Cedar Rapids, .42 (400)	*Orlando, .42*
Durham, .51 (377)	Savannah, .47 (416)
Glendale, .47	Sunnyvale, .64
Hampton, .60	Vallejo, .51
Huntsville, .49	Winston-Salem, .44

- High activism (>.39), high distress (1–364)

Canton, .42 (36)	Peoria, .67 (278)
Duluth, .60 (189)	Portsmouth, .69 (144)
Evansville, .56 (267)	Reading, .42 (146)
Lansing, .51 (218)	South Bend, .47 (260)
Miami Beach, .62 (244)	Springfield, Mo., .55 (357)
Oxnard, .40 (166)	

- Low activism (0–.39), high distress (1–364)

Beaumont, .33 (254)	Inglewood, .38 (149)
Decatur, .24 (99)	Providence, .27 (194)
Green Bay, .24 (348)	*Springfield, Ohio, .33 (81)*

- Low activism (0–.39), low distress (365–729)

Alexandria, .38	*Boise, .22*
Amarillo, .35	Clearwater, .22
Bloomington, .31	Dearborn, .31

Independence, .30   Santa Monica, .20
Lafayette, .29 (375)   Stamford, .24
Lakewood, .29   Tempe, .09
Little Rock, .38   Topeka, .29
Raleigh, .35   Tyler, .20
Santa Barbara, .09

We endeavored to select cities from all census regions (see figure 1.1). One city is located in the Northeast (Lowell); three are in the South (Beaumont, Huntsville, and Orlando); four are in the Midwest (Duluth, Evansville, Independence, and Springfield); and two are in the West (Boise and Santa Barbara). Our hope was, further, to select cities whose jurisdictional boundaries were not contiguous with other major cities and that were also somewhat isolated from major population centers. By doing so, we believed that we could better capture the impacts of a specific development project in our medium-sized cities without being overly concerned about the spillover effect of a neighboring (larger) city's development efforts. The inclusion of Independence and Lowell is an exception to that requirement.

Prior to our site visits, we contacted city officials asking for access to documents, files, notes, minutes of meetings, and other information, as well as for interviews. These previsit contacts allowed us to identify and replace jurisdictions that were reluctant to participate (three cities initially contacted declined to participate). The ultimate set of 10 cities contains places that are both similar and diverse. The cities fall within a common population range and are of the same metropolitan type, yet they vary in regional location, level of distress, and economic development activism. While we do not claim that any one of these cities is the archetypal American city, we do contend that, as a whole, the group is reasonably representative of medium-sized American communities.

Site Visits

Each author spent a week in five of the cities during 1988 and 1989. Nearly 100 interviews were conducted with city leaders, or approximately 10 city officials per city. Those interviewed were at least one elected official (mayor or councilor), the city manager (in cities with a council-manager form of government), the planning and development director, the finance officer, and other appointed officials (e.g., downtown devel-

Figure 1.1 The Location of the Study Cities.
Note: Circles indicate cities with populations greater than 250,000.

opment authority directors) who had economic development responsibilities. The following questions were asked:

- What is your vision for the future of your city? Define the good society as it applies to your city.

- What cities look to your city for leadership or as a model for development?

- What city would you like your city to emulate? Does it emulate that city adequately? What other cities does your city aspire to be most like? What cities does your city compete against regionally and nationally?

- Did the project accomplish what it was intended to do at the time the project was initiated? How do you judge whether or not a development project has succeeded? That is, what performance criteria do you employ? Define success and failure. How successful has the project been in generating revenue?

- Do you view the city as an investor in or an expediter of projects or as a subsidizer of private development? Why?

- What were the intended outcomes of the development project? What other goals did the project try to accomplish? What prior policy decisions were in force?

- Compared with other city-sponsored development projects, assess this project in terms of its level of uncertainty (high, medium, low), risk (high, medium, low), and the value of city investment (high, medium, low).

- How has the city skyline changed as a result of the project?

- Explain how land use, development mix, and density were affected by the project.

- What spillover effects have you seen as a result of the project? For example, have sales picked up? Have more people been attracted to the area for residential or commercial purposes?

- Who benefited from the project? Has the project engendered a change in the class of users? How?

Interviews with city officials and the materials provided by them were supplemented by interviews with other local leaders. These included developers, Chamber of Commerce officials, regional Council of Government personnel, university researchers, and newspaper editors. These noncity sources were especially helpful in establishing the broader context in which the city's development activities occurred and in resolving conflicting interpretations of events.

A brief economic history of each study city is presented below. To understand the attitudes and behaviors of contemporary city leaders, a sense of where the city has been is essential. The city's distress indicator and its index of economic development activism were used to assign it to one of four cells. These cells are labeled *expansionist* (low distress, high activism), *survivalist* (high distress, high activism), *market* (high distress, low activism), and *maintenance* (low distress, low activism). These four city classifications are discussed in further detail in chapter 2. Expansionist cities include Orlando, Huntsville, and Lowell. In the survivalist group are Duluth and Evansville. The market cities include Beaumont and Springfield. In the maintenance category are Boise, Independence, and Santa Barbara. Classification was based on 1986–87 data. A city's classification can change if its ranking on either index changes (an issue we revisit in chap. 7).

THE CITIES

The three expansionist cities are considered first, followed by their two survivalist counterparts, the two market cities, and the three maintenance cities. Population and land area data for the cities for the period 1940 to 1990 can be found in appendix A.

Huntsville

Huntsville, Alabama, was incorporated in 1811 and was the site of the constitutional convention that formed the state. Throughout its first 130 years, Huntsville's fortunes were inextricably tied to the cotton industry; the area's first cotton gin and first cotton mill were established there. As for so many southern cities, Huntsville's growth and expansion were interrupted by the Civil War, and it took several decades for the city to regain its stride. Its claim to economic fame until the 1940s was cotton manufacturing.

The U.S. army announcement in the early 1940s that it would build a chemical weapons manufacturing plant on 40,000 acres southwest of the city took Huntsville in a direction from which it has not wavered. This Defense Department installation was followed by the Redstone Arsenal, which manufactured conventional munitions and artillery shells. In 1950, a team of rocket scientists, including 100 Germans led by Wernher von Braun, moved to Huntsville to develop the U.S. missile program. Their pioneering research and development efforts gave way to the Army Ballistic Missile Agency and the Marshall Space Flight Center, both located in Huntsville. Huntsville's ties to the Defense Department remain close. One of the strategic defense initiative's (Star Wars) research facilities is located in Huntsville. In addition, 58 Huntsville firms have government contracts related to the SDI. The book value of government defense installations in Huntsville exceeded $800 million in the late 1980s and the U.S. army employs about 20,000 soldiers and civilians. The city, through a carefully orchestrated effort, has attracted an array of defense-related firms to the city, including Boeing, Martin Marietta, Hewlett Packard, McDonnell Douglas, Rockwell International, Raytheon, Morton Thiokol, and Lockheed.

In 1950, Huntsville's population was 16,000 in a city measuring four square miles. After aggressive annexations, the city is now 160 square miles, and after several waves of in-migration, the population has reached

160,000. During the 1980s, Huntsville's economy outpaced the rest of the state; per capita income was relatively high, unemployment relatively low. In fact, *INC Magazine* has several times listed Huntsville as one of its top ten "hot spot" (entrepreneurial) cities.

The racial composition of Huntsville is 72 percent white, 25 percent black. A strong mayor-council structure governs the city; since 1988, all five council members have been elected from districts.

Lowell

The touchstone of the American industrial revolution, or the "second American revolution" as Lowellians refer to it, has to be the mill town of Lowell, Massachusetts, named for Francis Lowell. It was here in 1821 that a group of Bostonian capitalists decided to build an extensive power-loom textile factory system, after successfully operating three small textile mills along the Charles River at Waltham near Boston.[7] The 32-foot fall in the Merrimack River, known as Pawtucket Falls, had required a canal around it in the late 1790s, but no city was laid out. The location of the textile industry at the fault line of the river resulted in the first planned industrial city in America. Within three decades of its founding, Lowell became the world's largest producer of cotton textiles. Canals criss-crossed the city, providing water to the power looms. Today, the original 5.6-mile canal system still dominates the landscape of the city.

Lowell, located 25 miles northwest of Boston, was established on March 1, 1826, and was legally incorporated as the third city in Massachusetts in 1836. It boomed as a result of the textile industry, reaching 112,759 persons in 1920. Low wages in the American South and other parts of the world resulted in the near-dismantling of the textile industry in Lowell.[8] Between 1920 and 1970 nearly all the textile mills shut their doors or relocated. The 1990 census put the population at 103,439.

Few large U.S. cities besides Lowell (only East St. Louis, Newark, and Gary compare) have come as close to economic collapse and total nonexistence. Its decline began earlier than other industrial cities, it bottomed out earlier than others, and it began the painstaking process of rebuilding earlier than most. Even the expansionist years of World War II, which brought life to industrial cities around the country, was only a momentary high spot in the inexorable decline of Lowell's manufacturing base.[9] In 1975 unemployment approached 12 percent, nearly double the national average; ten years later it was around 3 percent, nearly half the national average.

Lowell, a city that is 81 percent white, has two minority groups of significant size: Asians compose 11 percent of the population, Hispanics 10 percent. As for governance, Lowell uses a council-manager structure in which all 13 council members are elected at large.

Orlando

Orlando, Florida, referred to by some as the city Mickey built, has become a virtual boom city since the opening of Walt Disney World in 1971. Originally the center of an agricultural region (orange groves) in the middle of Florida, Orlando has become a tourist mecca for the nation and the hemisphere. The Walt Disney Company—including Disney World, EPCOT, and Disney/MGM Studios—although located outside the Orlando city limits, is the largest employer in the area (nearly 36,000 employees) and, according to city officials, contributes most other business-related employment. Together with the success of other nearby tourist and entertainment industries (e.g., Universal Studios, Cypress Gardens, Sea World, and the Magic—a National Basketball Association franchise), Orlando ranks behind only New York City in number of hotel rooms (more than 64,000), and more than 15 million airline passengers arrive yearly.[10]

Although population growth in Orlando itself has not been as spectacular as in the metropolitan area, it has been impressive. The 1990 census put Orlando's population at 164,693, a 28.4 percent increase over the 1980 census, which in turn was a 29.6 percent increase over the 1970 population. The population in Orlando's metropolitan statistical area (MSA) increased more than 100 percent between 1970 (453,270) and 1990 (1,072,748). The resulting urban sprawl has resulted in enormous loss of agricultural land. Orange grove acreage in Orange County (one of the three counties composing the Orlando MSA) shrank from 56,000 to 25,000 between 1975 and 1985.[11]

Urban sprawl and massive migration have placed the Orlando MSA among the nation's hot spots. Transportation and infrastructure issues are thus at the top of the city's agenda. While tourists (approximately 25 million each year) infuse large volumes of cash into the local economy, a large portion of the labor market is employed by the low-paying tourist industry.[12] The median value of homes has skyrocketed, so affordable housing is out of the reach of most working families (whose members "work for the Mouse," as the locals say).

Orlando is 69 percent white, 27 percent black, and 9 percent Hispanic. A mayor and a six-member council govern the city.

Duluth

Nestled in a narrow two- to six-mile-wide band of picturesque country and bordered by Lake Superior on the east and steep bluffs on the west, Duluth, Minnesota, is a cozy, 67-square-mile industrial city of nearly 85,000 people. Its city limits resemble a fettuccine noodle pasted to the crescent shoreline of Lake Superior. The city owns nearly 11,000 acres of land within its boundaries reserved for recreation and enjoyment—not for development. In these parks are many fishable streams and creeks. A frontier city surrounded by open space, Duluth has the warmth and charm of an older city, the comfort of a small town, and the economic problems of a steel city.[13]

As the major port for the iron ore mines of Minnesota, Duluth's growth and prosperity are inextricably linked to the fate of the steel industry in places as far away as Cleveland and Pittsburgh. U.S. Steel built a steel plant in the western part of the city at the turn of the century; the company closed it in the mid-1970s. The city's population exceeded 100,000 in 1930 and remained relatively stable for the next four decades, peaking at 106,884 in 1960, according to the decennial census. With the decline of employment opportunities in the steel industry and heavy manufacturing in general, Duluth's population dropped to 92,811 by 1980 and to 85,493 by 1990.

Duluth's population is not racially diverse—96 percent of the residents are white. Native Americans are the largest racial minority (2%). A strong mayor-council structure has been in place since 1956. Of the nine members of the city council, four are elected at large, five represent districts.

Evansville

Evansville, Indiana, is located at a sharp bend in the Ohio River 126 miles downstream from Louisville, Kentucky. Its economic history, like that of most river towns, has been tied to the fortunes of the river, the verdant farmlands surrounding it, and the transportation grid connecting Evansville to the major markets of the South and the Midwest. Evansville was settled in the early 1800s and incorporated as a town in 1819 and as a city in 1847. Its mid-nineteenth-century economic boost resulted from the construction of the Wabash-Erie Canal, which reaches the Ohio River at Evansville. Over the next century, its population grew slowly and steadily but never reached or rivaled that of the other great Ohio River cities, such as Pittsburgh, Cincinnati, and Louisville.

On the eve of World War II, the city's population stood at 97,000; the entire county of Vanderburgh, within which Evansville is the only city, was 131,000. Military manufacturing—most notably, the P-38 aircraft factory—invigorated the economy of the relatively small city. Spin-off industries picked up the slack left by declines in military production after the war, and by the late 1940s, Evansville was producing refrigerators, automotive parts, and household appliances. By the 1950 census, the city's population had increased from the 1940 census by a third, to 129,000—where it stabilized (the 1990 census puts Evansville's population at 126,272).

While the unemployment rate in 1986 stood at 6.4 percent, compared with the national average of 7.0 percent, per capita income for Evansville residents was $10,048, nearly 7 percent below the national average of $10,797. In 1979, Evansville's per capita income was only 4 percent less than the national average. Much of the growing income disparity can be explained by the rapid decline in relatively high-paying manufacturing jobs. Between 1977 and 1982, manufacturing employment for this blue-collar city dropped 34 percent, compared with a decline of only 2.5 percent nationally. The employment decline in manufacturing was recouped by the more rapidly growing, but lower paying, retail trade sector, up 15.1 percent between 1977 and 1982.

Evansville's population is 90 percent white and 10 percent black. The city has a strong mayor form of government and nine elected city council members.

Beaumont

Beaumont, Texas, is a city of 119,000 located 85 miles east of Houston. Natural resources, especially water and oil, have traditionally been harnessed for their economic value. Beaumont grew up along the banks of the Neches River, 35 miles north of the Gulf of Mexico. Although it was chartered by the Republic of Texas in 1838, Beaumont came of age in the twentieth century. Two pivotal events made the difference. First, in 1900, a hurricane virtually destroyed Galveston, Texas's premier port city. Galveston's misfortune became Beaumont's gain. Beaumont city leaders extended the existing ship channel to the city's docks, an action that made Beaumont a deepwater port and, therefore, a contender for shipping business. In 1988, 4.7-million tons of cargo moved through the port of Beaumont.

Even more important was the second event, the discovery in 1901 of vast oil reserves in an area known as Spindletop, south of the city. Within a month, Beaumont's population tripled to 30,000, and a new economic raison d'etre emerged. Even after Beaumont lost its prominence as the center for oil drilling, it retained its role in oil processing and refining. In oil-hungry America, Beaumont became a charmed city. Even today, the basis of the area's economy is oil refining and petrochemicals. The Mobil, Chevron, and Texaco refinery complexes located in the Beaumont area represent more than 10 percent of the nation's total petroleum refining capacity.

Since 1970, Beaumont's population size has remained relatively unchanged, with approximately 119,000 inhabitants. During the Texas boom of the 1960s and 1970s, when the state's population increased 48.5 percent and Houston and Dallas, the state's largest cities, grew by 70 percent and 33 percent, respectively, Beaumont's population actually declined by 1 percent.

The dramatic downturn in the oil industry in the early 1980s rocked Beaumont. Unemployment rates reflect just how devastating it was: in 1984, the city's unemployment rate was 9.6 percent; the figure climbed to 11.6 percent in 1985; it reached 12 percent in 1986. The following year showed some improvement (10 percent), and by 1988, the unemployment rate dropped to its five-year low, 7.8 percent. Despite the improvement in the unemployment rate, evidence of a sick economy lingered. In 1985, the average selling price for a single-family home was $69,891; by 1988 the figure had dropped to $61,880. Phrases such as "slow but steady improvement" characterize assessments of the local economy. "Slow" is probably accurate—new residential construction dropped 48 percent in fiscal 1988, as the housing market sought to correct itself.

Beaumont is a racially mixed city: 55 percent white, 41 percent black, 4 percent Hispanic. The city operates with a council-manager form of government. The mayor and two council members are elected at large; four council members are elected from districts.

Springfield

Construction of the National Road is responsible for the first economic boom in Springfield, Ohio. Funds for the National Road were depleted in 1838, after the road had been completed to Springfield, and for the next 12 years, travel and trade from the eastern United States to the Midwest along the road (now U.S. 40) stopped in Springfield. During those years, businesses sprang up to service the westward migration, and Springfield rapidly grew prosperous. In 1850, the city was incorporated under the laws of the state.

Located 45 miles west of Columbus and 20 miles northeast of Dayton, Springfield did not share the locational characteristics of earlier industrial cities. A plentiful supply of water, a deep harbor, and access to vital raw materials, such as coal or sand, which were primarily responsible for the location of most early nineteenth-century cities, are generally not available in Springfield. The city's growth after the Civil War was notable. The manufacture of farm implements for the expanding Midwest soon outstripped the businesses designed to service National Road travelers. By 1880, manufacturing of the Champion reaper made Springfield the largest farm machinery producer in the country. In fact, a century ago Springfield's industrial output exceeded that of Chicago.

Since the 1970s, declining manufacturing employment in the industrial belt hit Springfield particularly hard. No high-technology industries replaced the emigrating firms, few corporate headquarters located there, and relatively high-paying, white-collar, service sector jobs did not increase at a rate sufficient to recoup the city's declining employment base. The financial and emotional hardships on families and the community were severe.[14]

Springfield's population increased by 10 percent during World War II, reached 78,508 in 1950, and continued to grow modestly in the 1960s. By 1970 the official count stood at 81,924 and then sharply declined to 72,563 in 1980. The 1990 census put Springfield's population at 70,487, slightly below its 1940 level of 70,662. Because of unemployment and lack of high-paying jobs, emigration has probably not yet been curbed.[15]

The unemployment situation in Springfield has yet to rebound from the disastrous decline earlier in the 1980s. In 1982, the unemployment rate was 16.2 percent, or two-thirds higher than the national average of 9.7 percent. By 1986 the situation had improved; nevertheless, unemployment stood at 8.3 percent, a fifth higher than the national average of

7 percent. Per capita income has been diverging from the national average since the mid-1960s. In 1974, Springfield's average per capita income was $4,012, having increased at an average annual rate of only 6 percent since 1969. The national average was $4,572 in 1974, which represents an annual average increase of 7.6 percent since 1969. Springfield's 1974 per capita income was 12 percent lower than the national average; in 1979, it was 14 percent lower than the national average; by 1985 (at $9,108) it was 16 percent lower than the national average ($10,797).

Springfield is 82 percent white, 17 percent black. A council-manager structure, with a mayor and four council members, governs the city.

Boise

When the *New York Times Magazine* featured Boise, Idaho, in a recent article, a sidebar read "Potatoes aside, Idaho's isolated capital boasts an improbable bumper crop of major corporations."[16] That is one of the surprises of this city—not its potato production, not its isolation, not its role as state capital. Boise is a corporate center. One Fortune 500 firm, Boise Cascade (forest products), is headquartered there; and Morrison-Knudsen (a construction firm), Albertson's (a supermarket chain), Micron Technology (a microprocessor firm) also call Boise home. The largest manufacturing facility of Hewlett-Packard (a computer firm) outside of Silicon Valley is in Boise. Each of these corporations employs between 1,000 and 3,000 persons.

The same article calls Boise "an island of prosperity." Its population is highly educated: 83.4 percent have completed 12 or more years of schooling. Per capita income in 1985 was $11,740, with only 8.8 percent of its population falling below the poverty line. (Comparable statistics for the state of Idaho show 73.7 percent completing 12 years or more of school, a per capita income of $8,567, with 12.6 percent of the population below the poverty line.) There is little racial diversity in Boise—96.8 percent of the population is white. Beyond manufacturing and electronics, Boise's economy is bolstered by the presence of the state government, Boise State University, a large national guard contingent, and the medical industry. The city's employment base, dominated by wholesale and retail (25.3%), service (21.4%), and government (18.8%) sectors, grew 5.2 percent from 1987 to 1988. Unemployment has characteristically been low, ranging between 3.1 percent and 4.7 percent in the late 1980s.

Boise, with a 1990 population of 125,738, is located in southwestern Idaho and is the dominant city in the state. The city has a strong mayor-council form of government, with six council members elected at large.

Independence

Independence, Missouri, is the only city of the 10 in the sample that is not a central city. Over time, Independence has become a suburb of Kansas City. However, Independence was once a premier jumping off point for westward migration. In the mid-nineteenth century, the city bustled with economic activity. However, the road to regional greatness proved bumpy. An adjacent community to the west, Kansas City, was located on the banks of the Missouri River and offered water routes that were unavailable to Independence. In addition, Kansas City politicians recognized the direct benefits of economic growth and enacted measures to promote it. As a consequence, Independence retreated; it became a second-tier city within the region, although it remains the seat of Jackson County. Independence contains approximately 8 percent of the metropolitan Kansas City population. The city's population leveled off in 1970 and, since then, has been stable at about 112,000 residents.

Employment in Independence represents 5 percent of the total jobs in metropolitan Kansas City. Four of the city's firms have 500 or more employees: Olin Corporation (a small arms and ammunitions plant), Independence Regional Health Center, Deutz-Allis (formerly Allis Chalmers), and Medical Center of Independence. That Independence is not the economic hub of the region is evident when the city's figures are compared to areawide figures. From 1980 to 1985, employment in the Kansas City metropolitan area grew by 7 percent and the number of business establishments increased by 23 percent. The comparable numbers for Independence are 5 percent and 3 percent, respectively.[17] One estimate puts the number of residents commuting out of the city to work elsewhere in the 65–70 percent range.

There is not much racial diversity in Independence. The city is 96 percent white, 2 percent black. A council-manager structure governs the city, with the mayor and two council member elected at large and four council members elected from districts.

Santa Barbara

Santa Barbara is an oceanside California city of 85,571, nestled against the Santa Ynez Mountains. It is grappling with tremendous growth pressures. The city's own press releases refer to it as "one of America's most attractive and livable cities." Maintaining its attractiveness and livability is the ultimate goal of official Santa Barbara. As a result, the city embraces a second-generation growth management, emphasizing resource balance and self-sufficiency. Located 100 miles north of Los Angeles, the 18.6-square-mile city faces problems characteristic of a subset of coastal, Sun Belt cities caught in the crest of the latest development wave.

Santa Barbara traces its history to the Spanish settlements of the late eighteenth century. A military fortress was established there in 1782; a mission was founded four years later. Much of the city retains a distinct Spanish-Moorish style. Whitewashed stucco, red-tiled roofs, flowering courtyards, and palm-lined paseos provide the Santa Barbara "look." The city was incorporated in 1850 and reincorporated in 1899. It is the largest city in Santa Barbara County. The city's population grew 60–70 percent in the early decades of the twentieth century, 20–30 percent in the post–World War II period, and since 1970 less than 10 percent each decade. The slowdown in growth can be directly attributed to actions taken by Santa Barbara officials.

Santa Barbara's economy is healthy and is based primarily in services and retail sales. The largest private employers inside the city limits are a hospital, the telephone company, and a department store. Located nearby, but outside the city limits, are the University of California, Santa Barbara, and several high-technology enterprises such as Hughes, Delco, and Raytheon. Tourism has long been an important component of the local economy. In 1887, the Southern Pacific Railroad linked Santa Barbara to Los Angeles; in 1901, the rail system was completed northward to San Francisco. This opened Santa Barbara to tourism as wealthy East Coast residents flocked to the new "American Riviera." Although rail traffic has declined, tourists still find the city easily accessible via the Santa Barbara Airport and U.S. Highway 101.

Figures for the 1980s show that the city's unemployment rate has consistently lagged behind both the national and state averages by at least 2 percentage points. In the late 1980s, unemployment in the city was in the 4 percent range. Labor supply is a matter of concern for city leaders. Some fear that a lack of affordable housing in Santa Barbara and long commuting distances may cut the labor supply to such a degree that the economy will suffer.

Santa Barbara is 77 percent white, with Hispanics the largest minority group at 17 percent. Blacks and Asians each compose approximately 2 percent of the population. The city is governed through a council-manager system, with all six council members and the mayor elected at large.

2 / PUBLIC CAPITAL,

SYSTEMS OF CITIES,

AND PERCEPTUAL ORBITS

CITIES, LIKE any social organization, are constantly becoming or, more precisely, emerging. The old city dies, in a figurative sense, and a new one takes its place. Critical elements in transforming an old urban landscape into the cityscape of tomorrow are the vision of the city's leaders, their commitment to pursuing that vision, and their capacity to mobilize public capital for its attainment. The strength, diversity, and resiliency of the local economic base are also important. Urban economic development policy lies at the intersection of the city's political and economic realms. Changes in either of these sectors profoundly affect the other. City governments control land (or space) and have little control over labor and capital, yet all are necessary ingredients for a city's becoming the cityscape of the next millenium.

Changes in cities' built environment occur with at least the city governments' tacit endorsement and, in many instances, their active participation. City governments are increasingly involved in enhancing—even exploiting—the development potential of their territories.[1] If there is consensus among urban scholars, it is that cities have an interest in promoting economic development; that the intervention of city government in the development process profoundly affects the spatial and temporal dimensions of urban development; that market forces in and of themselves do not fully explain urban development patterns; and that politics matters in the direction, duration, and development of urban space.[2] The spatial implications of private capital investment decisions and individual decisions to migrate are not the only, and probably not the most important, determinants of cityscapes. City-sponsored economic development projects—that is, projects that have been invested in as a result of a political decision—alter a city's panorama in important ways.

Because these are city-sponsored projects, politics matters. That politics matters tells us little except that city government and public officials play a part in the development process. How politics matters requires an understanding of local officials' subjective interpretation of their objective environment.[3] Scholars of economic development, public finance, and public budgeting have focused on the composition of the public sector's wealth—or the supply of tools and techniques at the city's disposal.[4] None of them, however, has examined adequately either (1) the process by which city officials select the appropriate bundle of tools from this supply and offer them to developers or (2) what motivates their selection. We have found neither adequate data nor an appropriate model to show how government behavior is intended to change the urban environment. Harold Wolman reports, for example, that "very little systematic information exists on how public officials think about local economic development and how they make policy decisions in that realm."[5] This is not to say that the behavior of city officials or the reified city has not been studied, but there is a dearth of behavioral studies on city development decisions.[6] This book intends to fill that gap.

MOBILIZING PUBLIC CAPITAL

The following is an overview of our conceptual framework of the way public capital is mobilized to influence development.[7] *Public capital* is defined as the wealth and authority that is available to city government to produce more wealth. It denotes not only monetary resources or investments but anything of value, tangible or intangible, available for development purposes. Public capital is the collection of policy instruments that city governments have at their disposal to encourage, control, or complement development. *Mobilization* refers to the sequential process of selection, packaging, and utilization of those resources. These instruments include a variety of cost-reduction tools (e.g., tax incentives, land writedowns, and venture capital funds) and capacity-improving techniques (e.g., infrastructure improvements, land assemblage, and strategic planning).[8] They vary in their cost and complexity, in their adaptability and visibility, and in financial risk.[9] City officials select from among these instruments to direct, mold, and otherwise influence development.

When do city governments venture into the development milieu and mobilize public capital for development? The two key factors in understanding city development behavior are (1) city officials' acceptance of the position of the city within its relevant system of cities and (2) the city's tax-service equilibrium. The centrality of these factors does not mean that other explanations are unimportant but, rather, that other explanations are subsumed within these two overarching considerations.[10] Both, of course, are conditioned by external political and economic forces and by local fiscal policies.

Aspirations and the System of Cities

The concept of a hierarchy among cities argues that cities within a specified region specialize in producing goods and services for that region. The more economic diversification, the more dominant a city is in its region's system of cities. Each region is dominated by a primate city—a city functionally superior to all other cities within the region. The arrangement of cities in this hierarchical system of cities depends upon a number of economic factors, including land availability, cost of capital and labor, and most important for regional economists, transportation costs. City-hierarchy analysis overlooks the crucial influence and critical role of the city government in altering a variety of costs that would change a city's position within its system of cities.[11] In sum, the political variable is absent.

Theory notwithstanding, city officials are extremely active in promoting development in their city. Surely part of the impetus to promote development reflects economic downturns and a city's fragile fiscal position, as we argue in the next section. Yet city activism in the development arena also reflects a political vision of the city's position in its system of cities, whether this vision is held by a majority of the residents or even by a minority of the business and financial community. City leaders are very conscious of where their city "fits."[12] City officials clearly feel development imperatives from other relevant cities, wherever those cities are situated geographically. They use those competitive cities' accomplishments as yardsticks against which to measure their city's economic promise and performance. Local government officials aspire to maintain or change their city's competitive position or rank within this relevant system of cities. Consequently, they, as the possessors of public authority in the community, take actions they believe will achieve this objective. A city's position within a system of cities is not a consequence of market forces and transportation costs only. (In fact, a discrete region may no longer be identifiable in the age of economic internationalization; a global system of cities cutting across regions and nations may be more descriptive today, especially as mayors publicly worry about losing industry and commerce to the Far East and elsewhere.) Rather, the aspirations and visions of local leaders, especially those responsible for a city's development, are influential in assessing a city's position within its (perhaps redefined) system of cities.[13]

Answers to the questions, Where do we fit? and Where would we like to be? are articulated by city officials, both elected and appointed, and guide their bargaining with developers. These local leaders ultimately decide which development tools to use to approximate their collective vision of what the city can become. This process represents the leadership's subjective interpretation of where the city ought to be heading.[14] And those visions are not immutable; they change and evolve.

For example, in many metropolises, the central business district is no longer the only center of economic and commercial activity. Smaller clusters of business activity have emerged in the form of scaled-down and manageable business districts, or "urban villages."[15] Many large cities have turned their promotional activities away from selling the advantages of the dense central city to stressing the livability of their urban villages. Citing the blossoming of new centers of commercial and residential activity, Philip Langdon writes approvingly of the new planning that "puts more emphasis on an appealing urban streetscape with well-defined streets, squares, and parks. Along the East River in the Borough of Queens, [two design firms] are laying out a seventy-acre project, which includes housing, offices, shops, and recreation facilities, on a regular street grid."[16] Zoning, infrastructure, and other incentives are provided in many cities in an effort to foster the development of urban villages. In a recent publication, Joel Garreau argues that clusters of commercial activity on the edges of cities have given metropolises a certain identity or image outside the more popular view held of, and by, the central city.[17] The image of these "edge cities" stands in sharp contrast to the image of the central city. Edge-city growth, development, and acceptance, just like that of their central-city siblings, depends on the public's willingness to provide infrastructure, tax abatement, land, and other development tools controlled by local officials.

Aspirations—images of the preferred future—take the form of economic development goals for a city. Under the titles of "job creation" and "downtown revitalization," public dollars underwrote development projects around the country throughout the 1980s. Economic development was conceived as a competitive venture, a means of keeping up with, or getting ahead of, other cities. Just as development projects may generate revenues for the city, these projects are often tangible symbols of survival, transformation, or ascendance, depending on the city's circumstances. In other words, they have important image-creation value.

The Tax-Services Equilibrium

A city's mobilization of public capital to influence development is not simply a matter of aspirations, visions, and the system of cities. City governments, as social organizations, search for an equilibrium in their relations with the external environment. Given that city governments operate within fixed territorial jurisdictions and that capital is not similarly constrained, they must try to maximize service output within an acceptable tax effort. Mark Schneider, in an elaboration of what he calls the service-tax ratio, argues that "the desire for more services without higher local taxes or for the same services at lower taxes clearly motivates the behavior of key actors in communities. Because a stronger tax base improves the local service/tax ratio, the pursuit of [a] tax base emerges as a core goal in local politics."[18]

City fiscal systems are structured within such constraints as the level of political participation, the demand for services, and the politically acceptable tax limits. In each community, a satisfactory (although not an abstractly optimal) balance is reached through the political process. Even city governments in which income redistribution is a primary policy objective, such as Cleveland during the mayoral term of Dennis Kucinich, are constrained from venturing too far toward that objective and thus endangering the balance.[19] Moving beyond the acceptable limit will likely result in disinvestment and withdrawal of credit. Therefore, tax and service levels rise and fall within a dynamic equilibrium. Disequilibrium results when service delivery declines, when the price of service delivery increases, or when perceived opportunities for more efficient and higher-quality service delivery are present. The most visible disruption to the tax-services equilibrium occurs when a city's tax base shrinks as the local economy sours.

When the city's fiscal system no longer delivers a politically acceptable quantity of goods and services at a politically acceptable tax price, city officials engage in "problemistic" search for a way to respond to this disequilibrium.[20] City officials must then decide to exercise local powers. These powers can be separated into two distinct classes: (1) the authority to claim scarce resources and (2) the political will to exercise such authority. The reason city officials tend not to exercise their full authority—the issue of political will—is that the exercise of authority is in constant tension with the actions and policies of competing cities within a federal system and with their own vision of their city's role in the development process. A city government's will is checked by Tieboutian forces that encourage cities not to develop revenue and expenditure structures wildly out of line with those of competing cities. To do so would risk losing population and the tax base as people and firms find it advantageous to migrate.[21] Paul Peterson, Barry Rabe, and Kenneth Wong identify a number of development activities (such as infrastructure and police protection) and argue that "of course, all these services must be purchased efficiently so that local taxes remain competitive with those in communities providing comparable services. And the appropriate mix of taxes and services depends on the geographic and social context in which the community finds itself."[22]

Important to our argument about the tax-services equilibrium is that (1) efforts to restore the equilibrium are rooted in a city's development function and (2) the decision to mobilize a development tool is anchored in a tax-services disequilibrium and fundamentally unrelated to employment and income issues. The literature on economic development outcomes frequently identifies and measures the employment-generating or personal-income-enhancing effects of a city's development projects, as if those effects were the salient and overriding concerns in the decision calculus. A community in which only retired, nonworking folk reside would not trigger a search for development incentives as long as the current revenue stream matched service delivery costs or needs. Therefore, measuring the number of jobs generated or income produced by development projects has had the effect of shifting the analytical focus from the intended outcome. As a consequence of this shift, a project can be proclaimed a success by city officials and urban analysts to the extent that employment has increased—even if employment in one city increased at the expense of lost employment in another city, thus increasing net employment by nothing. Our perspective is that only if the public fisc is healthier or restored to previous conditions of balance can success be proclaimed, that is, success in restoring the equilibrium. City behavior is designed to address the tax-services equilibrium, not the number of persons employed.

This is not to say that a city of unemployed would be no cause for alarm; it would be. Rather, increasing the employment base is not the motivating force behind city officials' decisions to engage in the development process; an inability to deliver services at a competitive tax rate is.

The Trigger to Action

Social organizations prefer to control and manipulate their own environments, to resist change and tension, and to adjust to new situations in order to survive. As social organizations, cities continually adapt to their constantly changing environments. External and internal stimuli, catalysts, and impulses are ingested and translated into programs and policies by key city officials. Richard Cyert and James March contend that all social organizations respond to such stimuli by searching for solutions to the perceived problems; the hoped-for result of that search is the reestablishment of a steady state, or an equilibrium.[23] Likewise, a city engages in problemistic search for the appropriate response to the city's need to survive, to thrive, and to reestablish a balance.[24] In particular, the equilibrium that cities seek to maintain is between their revenue-generating capacity and their service delivery needs.[25] Nevertheless, organizations, and cities in particular, do not adapt automatically to changing environments. Rather, the city's leaders make conscious and public decisions about whether or not to respond to changes, about the extent the city's resources should be invested in the response, and about the objectives of such capital mobilization efforts.

Threats to a city's revenue stream disrupt the tax-services balance and most assuredly trigger the search for a development policy to redress the imbalance. A second trigger mechanism is perceptual; city officials may want their city to move into a higher orbit or plane within the relevant system of cities. In these instances, city leaders hope to expand their city's influence beyond the immediate spatial and economic region and prefer not to leave that shift to the marketplace. They actively intervene in hopes their city will catapult to a higher level or regain lost status and return to a former level within its system of cities.

Based on the sequential ordering of events identified in figure 2.1, we

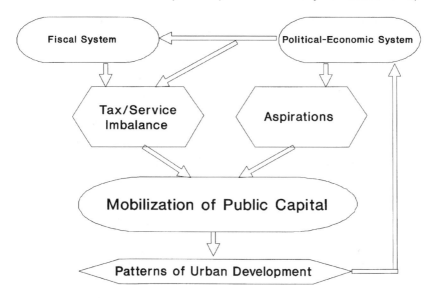

Figure 2.1. The Tax-Services Equilibrium Model

expect officials in fiscally stressed cities to become active promoters of development in order to recoup lost ground and reclaim their prior equilibrium position. Officials respond to the pressure of fiscal stress either by actively promoting development or by not doing so.[26] Fiscally strained cities whose officials do not become actively engaged in the development process, for whatever reason, face the possibility of drastic downsizing. Likewise, officials in fiscally healthy cities also have choices, but it is their aspirations for the city that trigger the mobilization of public capital, not a fiscal imbalance. If they have grand plans—visions of moving to a new plane—then they will actively promote development. If they are content with the city's position, then they are not likely to mobilize capital for development.

A city government's orientation reflects its leaders' aspirations and its tax-to-services equilibrium. In what we label *survivalist* cities, decisions are triggered by a tax-services imbalance. In *market* cities that suffer economic and fiscal stress, officials leave the city's economic fortunes to the private marketplace. The trigger for *expansionist* cities is the desire to become a higher-order city. For *maintenance* cities, the trigger is city officials' desire not to alter the city's position within the system of cities but, rather, to control or manage growth.

City officials' behavior can change as the trigger mechanisms change. Fiscal stress varies over time; aspirations may also vary. A maintenance city may become an active promoter of growth and development (and thus expansionist) upon the displacement of the no-growth coalition by a progrowth set of actors.[27] The changing fiscal fortunes of a city are likely to produce different motivations for government involvement in the local economy. The local government in Houston, which embraced an expansionist philosophy during the 1960s and 1970s, began to sound more like a survivalist city government in the 1980s.[28] As triggers change, orientations shift, and that is reflected in the mobilization of public capital.

City officials agree to intervene in the marketplace for reasons other than enhancing the efficiency of an abstract, spaceless market. Territory matters, and as a consequence, what city officials look for in development projects may appear rather perverse in an economic sense. Success is seldom defined in economically efficient terms. Development projects are undertaken by cities either to generate revenue (as an investor) or to address some particular aspect of market failure as it is defined in a spatial context of the city's jurisdictional limits (as a subsidizer-expediter). Whether the investment is efficient or optimal according to one's definition of investment objectives is not always relevant to the decision to subsidize a particular project. To assess a project's success with such a viewpoint becomes meaningless. Rather, a project's performance in addressing the specific market failure identified by officials at the time the project was undertaken is the benchmark by which success or failure should be measured. Likewise, optimal return on investment for city projects designed to generate revenues becomes a less useful standard against which to measure success than city officials' revenue-generating benchmark. Definitions of success and failure depend on city space and officials' motives.

Cities exist in a network of other cities, small and large, proximate and distant. Yet this system of cities is not immutable. New cities emerge, old cities fade. A city is not forever locked into second- or third-tier status. Below, we explore the system of cities, both from a central-place theoretic angle and from the perspective of city officials. We contend that city leaders' perceptions of their city's place, or orbit, and of their city's systemic competition directly influence that city's economic development policy. In effect, city officials redefine the relevant system of cities. Local officials take actions that reflect the aspirations they have for their city in that redefined system.

CENTRAL-PLACE THEORY:
THE CONVENTIONAL WISDOM

Economic theories purporting to explain urban growth touch only a few aspects of urban development and often ignore the complex interactions of social and cultural phenomena. A city's development, according to the noted urban and regional scientist Harry Richardson, "cannot be explained solely in economic terms."[29] Yet, the most influential approaches to understanding urban growth and development and to prescribing policy responses derive from the economics discipline. One of the more important and widely understood approaches adopted by economists as well as geographers is central-place theory, in which "central places are defined as centers where activities locate in order to serve a market area."[30]

In central-place theory, urban centers serve areawide markets; the larger the urban center, the larger the area served by the central place. City hierarchy argues that cities within a specified region specialize in producing goods and services for that region. The more economic diversification, the more dominant a city is in its region's system of cities. Each region is dominated by a primate city, or a city that is functionally superior to all other cities within the region. The resulting pattern of cities can be visualized as a hierarchical pyramid, in which some cities occupy the same place within the hierarchy and are subordinate to some cities and superior to others. In other words, the "central place principle has a . . . well-defined hierarchy [within a system of cities] wherein (i) all places on the same level are functionally identical and (ii) higher level places export all the bundles of goods provided by lower level places plus a distinctive bundle of their own."[31] The arrangement of cities in this hierarchical system of cities depends upon a number of economic factors, including land availability, the cost of capital and labor, and most important for regional economists, transportation costs. Central places vary in size (population) and market area served (space). Empirical studies on urban agglomeration economies and transportation costs dominate the specific approach of scholars who subscribe to the tenets of central-place theory.

Nevertheless, all economists do not accept central-place theory. As a mental construct, many economists and urban planners find it useful, but when the assumptions are subject to critical analysis, the theory pales.[32] The celebrated developer of central-place theory, Walter Christaller, identifies a set of assumptions that include an evenly distributed population over a homogeneous area, uniform production costs, and identical consumer product preferences across space. "Central places are sited in a pattern which maximises the spacing of places, subject to the constraint that all available space is swallowed up in at least one market area."[33] In other words, central places of higher orders dominate entirely the markets of lower-order places. The notion of agglomeration economies is useful to understand in explaining city hierarchies. Agglomeration economies refer to the spatial proximity of producers (especially interdependent firms) to one another in order to exact savings in transportation costs, scale economies (associated with, for example, technology and management specialists), labor specialization, and other factors.

Based on these assumptions, the spatial configuration of cities resembles hexagonal or honeycomb-shaped market areas, in which each city has a place. The products produced by a lower-order city are consumed within its market area; consumers within that market area also consume goods produced in higher-order cities that are not produced in lower-order cities. Consequently, overlapping hexagonal market areas cover all available space. The rank of any city, then, depends on the number of functions or activities it provides. This in turn suggests that a city's population, as a surrogate measure for number of functions, will vary directly with the hierarchical order of the central place. As a consequence, higher-order cities have larger populations and more functions than lower-order cities and tend to be equally spaced vis-à-vis other higher-order cities. Within the hierarchical distribution of cities, then, are a number of medium-sized cities with specialized functions. These cities are spaced closer together than higher-order cities. Many smaller-sized cities and towns within the orbits of these medium-sized cities provide limited services. In other words, "orders of towns with more complex sets of activities will possess all the central activities of lower orders plus a group of central activities that will distinguish them from the central places of immediately lower order."[34]

One critique of this approach is that, although these assumptions and the resulting patterns of market areas might be useful in explaining urban development on uninhabited and generally level terrain, it would not explain urban development in most regions of the world. Indeed, the theoretical precursor to central-place theory was Heinrich von Thünen's classic nineteenth-century study of transportation costs and the spatial development of cities in the sparsely populated areas of the American upper Midwest.[35] Walter Christaller, in 1933, then developed the theoretical support for the well-known city hierarchy and provided empirical referents from southwest Germany. Moreover, central-place hierarchy has been criticized because it ignores the distorting effects of geography and geology (rivers and harbors, especially) and transportation networks on place, city size, market areas, and location. It also seems particularly unsuited to explain urban development patterns in highly urbanized regions, such as New York City and Chicago. In these dense metropolitan areas, market areas of similar places overlap and are not clearly delineated, and some do not fall within the orbit of higher-order places.[36]

In addition, central-place theory may have lost some of its temporal relevance, since a rapid alteration of the relative economic positions of American cities is occurring.[37] Many once-dominant cities have been eclipsed economically by formerly subordinate cities, due to the macro-level restructuring of the national economy away from long-established manufacturing sectors toward newer industries based on information processing, electronics, and bioengineering.[38] In addition, the mushrooming of the service sector has wreaked havoc on many local economies. Some observers argue that the ascension of formerly peripheral places has created a newly differentiated urban hierarchy.[39] Just as the industrial revolution established a new hierarchy, the decentralization of industry is generating still another. The changing economy has contributed to the alteration of urban space. The metropolis is becoming a polycentric urban field, rather than one dominated by a primate city.[40]

Central-place theory, despite its limitations, has had some practical applicability. Brian Berry, in his work with the Economic Development Administration in the 1960s and 1970s, devised a hierarchy for each of 173 EDA-defined economic areas called "daily urban systems."[41] These areas were derived from commuting patterns around economic centers. The highest level is occupied by the metropolis, the next level by wholesale-retail cities. Following them in order are complete shopping cities, partial shopping cities, and full-convenience center cities. The criteria for the levels are based on the functional size and complexity of the city and the degree to which "nesting" occurs, that is, the dependence of lower-level centers upon higher-level centers. In another extension of central-place theory, Rand McNally subdivided the nation into a series of major and basic trading areas. The 494 basic trading areas are derived from factors such as physiography, population, newspaper circulation, economic activities, highway facilities, railroad service, suburban transpor-

Figure 2.2 The Economic Ranges of the Study Cities

tation, and field reports of experienced sales analysts.[42] Basic trading areas agglomerate into 50 "major trading areas."

The EDA and Rand McNally formulations can be applied to the cities in our study. With the exception of Independence, which was not in Berry's categorization, the cities are wholesale-retail, or second-order, places. Figure 2.2 reflects the economic ranges, adapted from Rand Mc-Nally's basic trading areas for the ten cities. (Lowell and Independence do not have distinctive trading areas, embedded as they are in the economies of Boston and Kansas City, respectively.) Perhaps the most notable aspect of these second-tier cities is the relatively modest economic shadow they cast, in terms of conventional central-place theory.

To the extent that central-place theory informs conceptualizations of urban economic growth, it leaves precious little room for the visible hand of city government. Indeed, except for the presumption that governments distort the machinations of the marketplace, the assumptions that undergird urban hierarchy analysis give almost no role to city governments except as they respond to the demands of the marketplace: city governments are expected to be responsive to firms that locate within a city. But central-place theory (since it is rooted in the economics of comparative advantage, which in effect emphasizes market prices of land, labor, raw materials, capital, and transportation), ignores or at least minimizes the potential importance of city governments' abilities to alter relative prices. As a factor influencing a city's comparative advantage, government incentives receive little attention or analysis. A city's proactive economic development function is anathema to the mainstream of urban-hierarchy analysis.

POLITICS AND THE SYSTEMS OF CITIES

Urban-hierarchy analysis is constantly being revised and refined in the literature on urban growth, but even these revisions neglect the critical role of city government in altering costs designed to change a city's position within its system of cities. Economists' approaches tend to discount the influence of any nonmarket development on a city's place in the hierarchy. Yet real world examples abound of the transformational effect of nonmarket forces on local economies. Thus, two important political modifications should be included in the conventional central-place theoretic framework of market supply and demand forces, agglomeration economies, and regularity in the spatial distribution of places. The first modification is a requirement to examine the perceptions, attitudes, and actions of urban policymakers in pursuing their vision of the good society (even when that action violates economic niceties of efficiency). In other words, an examination of political behavior must be introduced. The second modification is the structural or constitutional arrangement of roles, responsibilities, and authorities of overlapping government units; that is to say, federalism and intergovernmental relations matter. Political behavior is addressed in the next section; a discussion of federalism follows it.

Perceptions and Political Behavior

When city officials speak of aspiring to be the next success story (the next Charlotte, the next Phoenix), the portrait they are painting is not too unlike the conventional city hierarchy. These statements acknowledge their city's influence on the immediate spatial and economic region; their hope however is that regional boundaries and their city's influence within it will expand. In sum, these officials want their lower-order city to become a higher-order city. But, in many cities, it is not enough to leave these aspirations to the workings of the marketplace. City officials actively intervene in hopes of moving their city to a higher level in their hierarchy.[43]

City leaders' perceptions of their city's place in its hierarchy and their perception of competition among levels of the hierarchy may be more important than any empirically determined configuration based on spatial market areas. Market areas are contiguous, spatial regions, theoretically hexagonal in shape due to transportation costs from central places. Yet, empirically, central-place theory's predictive powers of urban location have been questioned, as a result of distorted transportation networks and other modifications of its underlying assumptions.[44] More recently, the spatial dominance of market areas by higher-order cities has been questioned because of the internationalization of capital and technology. Distant cities, rather than larger, highly specialized, and closer cities, now dominate the supply of certain goods to market areas of less-specialized areas. Foreign cities and cities in noncontiguous regions have become important in providing goods and services to market areas. Cities within those lower-order market areas, as a consequence, no longer develop and invest in commodities produced by the dominant city in the region; rather, competition to develop previously imported commodities ensues with other cities, often nonproximate.

City officials and development officers often claim they are in economic competition with some distant city (e.g., Lowell with Huntsville) rather than with a city of the same order in a contiguous region (e.g., Lowell with Providence, or Huntsville with Chattanooga). It becomes increasingly unimportant in today's society to know a city's geographic region in determining its competitors or its higher-ranked cities. Supplier cities have blurred into a set of regionally noncontiguous cities, the distinction between central places and "off-centered" places has become clouded.[45] City officials often pursue development policies that will lift their city to a higher-order plane within their relevant system of cities but not necessarily within the set of contiguous or proximate cities.

Cities in a Federal System

Federal and state constitutional, statutory, and other legal constraints influence the position of a city in its system. The constellation of U.S. cities would have been quite different had there been no federal interstate highway program or had federal housing programs not been skewed toward new suburban construction. During the 1980s, the federal government concentrated on national economic growth and global market shares while reducing concern for cities. As Carter's President's Commission for a National Agenda for the Eighties and President Reagan's *1982 National Urban Policy Report* made abundantly clear, the best medicine for city and regional economies was a strong national economy.[46] Programs directly aimed at community economic development encountered diminishing support as Congress struggled with the harsh realities of deficit reduction and the Gramm-Rudman-Hollings act. Big-city mayors, decrying what they termed "the massive disinvestment in America's cities and towns," found few sympathetic ears in the nation's capital. Hitting the cities especially hard in the 1980s was the termination of general revenue sharing in 1986 and of the urban development action grant program in 1987 and cutbacks in the community development block grant and economic development administration programs. Restrictions on industrial development bonds and the holding of substantial surpluses in the highway and transit funds rather than spending them further clouded cities' fiscal pictures, as the federal government gradually broke its fiscal links with cities.

While federal grants were drying up, federal regulatory action was relentless. More than half of all preemption statutes enacted since the founding of the Republic have been enacted since 1969—about 91 during Reagan's presidency alone.[47] The effect of these mandates is to exacerbate city fiscal problems and, more perniciously, to force cities to continue funding federal priorities while they simultaneously reduce (or eliminate) spending on their own priorities. The 1986 Tax Reform Act, for example, severely restricted issuance of tax-exempt development bonds. And even the costs of issuing general obligation bonds for basic infrastructure— cities' most often-used development tool—escalated in some cities because of the mandated "reporting requirements" of the new tax code.[48]

The Supreme Court sent mixed signals about the federal government's role in local governance and development policy, as well. In both the *Garcia v. San Antonio Metropolitan Transit Authority* and the *South Carolina v. Baker* decisions, the Court told state and local governments not to expect protection from the judicial process (the reserved clause of the Tenth Amendment).[49] Instead, the justices advised that grievances be taken through the political process, that state and local governments become "petitioners" to the Congress for protection.

Besides the constitutional concerns these federal actions raise are the costs to city governments, often in areas that cities would choose not to spend their own funds on; city government costs and expenditures escalate due to federal government mandates, but their revenues are increasingly derived only from the city's revenue-generating capacity. A city's revenue-generating capacity depends, in turn, on state-imposed city taxing authority as well as on its political will to raise revenues to support unfunded, federally mandated activities. The losers are the city's citizens, because their unique preferences and needs are sacrificed to the national will. As a consequence, promoting the local economy to refill the city's coffers and maintain (or expand) city service levels, then, becomes of paramount importance to city leaders. It is no wonder that the explosion in city development efforts in the 1970s and 1980s coincided with the federal government's encumbering of city revenues. City leaders' response to these federal actions is to continue funding city priorities while simultaneously meeting their federally imposed responsibilities.

Cities have had uneven relations with their state governments. Especially contentious have been conflicts over questions of local autonomy.[50] For example, cities and towns in Massachusetts and New Hampshire believed the Declaration of Independence shifted sovereign power to them, not to their states. After the American Revolution, cities did not always practice republican governance. Aldermen in some cities, for example, had life tenure and could select their successors (e.g., Norfolk and Annapolis).[51] As a new republican spirit swept the nation, challenges to these life-tenure aldermen were taken to state legislatures. By the mid-1850s, in response to perceived abuse of authority and unprecedented local corruption, states had extended their influence, in some cases to the point of assuming control over local police forces (e.g., in New York City, Detroit, Boston, Baltimore, St. Louis, and Kansas City).

The extension of state influence over local governments was succinctly proclaimed in 1868, when Judge John F. Dillon declared that "municipal corporations owe their origin to, and derive their power and rights wholly from, the legislature. It breathes into them the breath of life, without which they cannot exist. As it creates, so it may destroy. If it may destroy, it may abridge and control."[52] The situation was clear: if local governments wanted greater autonomy, they had to alter the state's incorporation statutes. One means for cities to remove themselves from the restrictive Dillon Rule was to adopt home rule, an option that by 1990 was in place in 47 states.[53] (Of the cities studied here, nine are located in states that grant home rule. Huntsville is the exception.)

With home rule and other extensions of municipal authority, municipal corporations carved out their political domains. Not only were municipalities required to provide services according to the state's directives under the incorporation statutes, they were also afforded the right to determine other legitimate activities, including the promotion of economic development. Cities could expand their development options from the traditional provision of basic infrastructure to more exotic and entrepreneurial activities, such as assembling land packages and granting tax deferrals. Keenly aware that financially distressed cities could upset the state's fiscal health, state governments in the 1980s began reexamining their annexation laws, tax policies, and regulations with an eye to local government impact. In an effort to spur development, many states invested in local infrastructure, created low-interest loan programs and venture capital funds, and established enterprise zones and small-business incubators.[54] In general, these actions expanded the options (and in some instances, the funding) available to city governments. Armed with these development tools and the legal authority to use them to enhance the development potential of the city, city leaders could prod their city toward their vision of the good society.

PERCEPTUAL ORBITS

The orbits of these cities from the perspectives of city leaders frequently differ from their location in a system rooted in central-place theory. When local officials were asked about competing cities—about the cities they aspired to become—their visions frequently stretched beyond these conventional economic systems. Local leaders might use proximate cities (especially hubs) as points of reference; however, they considered more distant cities (especially those reputed to be successful and worthy of emulation) part of their perceptual systems.

Such national thinking may have been instigated by footloose corporations. In selecting sites for investment and expansion, corporations typically inform competing cities about the locations they are considering. This may have forced cities to perceive competitor cities beyond a narrow band of "like" cities. In other words, corporations' influence on perceived competitors stretches city officials' realm of thinking beyond the proximate spatial area to a larger network, in which space and terri-

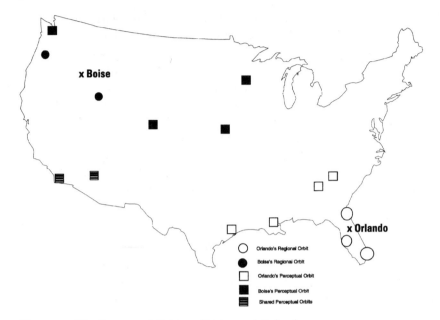

Figure 2.3. The Perceptual Orbits of Boise and Orlando

tory have little meaning. As officials ponder alternative strategies for development, these perceptual systems cities may have more relevance than
nearby political and economic systems.

We classify a city's perceptual orbit according to the views of city
officials. One is *cities with expanding orbits,* implying that the economic
base is strong and that city officials want their city to move up to the next
orbit and compete beyond the region. *Cities with self-contained orbits*
are cities whose economic base is also strong but whose officials are not
eager to change the city's orbit. *Cities with uncertain orbits* have a weakened economic base, and city officials encounter difficulty in influencing
the local economy. Officials in the first two orbits can control their destiny; officials in the third category are less successful. Figure 2.3 offers a
visual representation of how officials in two expanding orbit cities see
their geographical ranges.

Cities with Expanding Orbits

Boise is already the dominant city in Idaho, and its officials perceive an
expansive, far-flung realm. Boise made only modest use of development

tools throughout the mid-1980s. That, along with its low level of distress, placed Boise in the maintenance category of cities. However, by the time of our visit in 1989, Boise had replaced its long-time elected leadership with far more proactive officials. The city began to use development tools vigorously in pursuit of the new leaders' vision of what the city could become. (Boise's transition is discussed in chaps. 3 and 7.) Its geographical isolation has not caused the new city officials to think narrowly. Traditionally, Boise has looked in a northwesterly direction to the larger cities of Portland and Seattle. But with a new city administration in place, one with a development mandate from the voters, Boise has widened its gaze. Now officials unabashedly name Denver, Kansas City, Phoenix, Tucson, and larger California cities as legitimate competitors. In a classic case of thinking big, Boise's perceptual orbit extends beyond the intermountain West.

In Alabama, Huntsville sees itself overtaking Birmingham as the economic capital and eventually Montgomery as the political capital (if only in a de facto sense). But Huntsville, qualitatively different from other cities in the state, really does not use cities in the state as points of reference. Instead, Huntsville considers itself an equal partner in a high-technology-based system of mid-South cities anchored by Atlanta on the east and Memphis on the west. As for the cities that Huntsville uses as points of comparison, San Jose and Boston are frequently mentioned. That officials in Huntsville consider such far-flung cities as competitors is further confirmation of a specialized, national system.

Lowell—after nearly a half century of uninterrupted economic decline (save during World War II), as its textile mills moved to the South and overseas—began to reassert its development potential in the late 1970s. With strong political support from Councillor (and later Senator) Paul Tsongas, Congressman James Shannon, and City Manager Joseph Tully, among others, the city acted aggressively to resurrect its former status as a regional (if not national) economic center. Although nearby cities similar in size to Lowell (Portland [Maine], Salem, and Lawrence) might have seemed its logical competitors for investment, Lowell officials in the early 1980s had different ideas. As stated in the Lowell Plan, a blue print for promoting cooperation between the public and private sectors, Lowell was to become "the preeminent middle-sized city in America." City officials, especially those who sit on the board of directors of the Lowell Plan, Inc., and private-sector leaders aspired to make Lowell a more important economic actor than it ever was in the past and certainly more dominant within its relevant system of cities than before. Those with power in Lowell certainly did not believe that Lowell was positioned to challenge Boston's hegemonic position in its relevant system of cities in New England, nor that it ever would be; but Lowell's city officials no longer find that the city can, or should, be likened to cities that in the previous two decades easily could have been considered comparable cities. The relevant system of cities included competitive cities and urban regions of other high-technology corridors, including the Silicon Valley and Research Triangle and urban centers in the Far East.

Officials of Orlando, which has had extremely good fortune since Walt Disney selected a neighboring site a quarter century ago as its East Coast headquarters, continue to be optimistic about their city's growth. As a recreation and retirement mecca, the economic growth rate has yet to slow down. City officials believe that Orlando can become the dominant city or one of the dominant cities in the Southeast—and certainly in the rapidly growing state of Florida. Diversifying the city's image from Mickey's City they believe, will reap enormous profits. Consequently, the city invests heavily in low-risk development projects, to encourage even greater dominance in its system of cities. City officials are by no means willing to rely only on market mechanisms and private investment decisions to fuel their city's growth. They want to be partners in that process so that their regional competitors (Jacksonville, Atlanta, and Charlotte) and their more distant competitors (Phoenix and San Diego) might be challenged.

Cities with Self-contained Orbits

The city of Independence struggles to emerge from the large shadow cast by Kansas City. Independence remains the seat of Jackson County; however, satellite county offices in Kansas City dwarf those in Independence. Economically, Independence, once the dominant city in the area, was displaced as Kansas City flourished. Today, it seeks to become something other than a bedroom community, and there is some evidence that its strategy is having success. In 1970, approximately 75 percent of the employed population worked outside the city. By 1980, that percentage was between 65 and 70. Ironically, as Kansas City suffers the deconcentration fate that affects other large central cities, it is not Independence that is reaping the benefits. Instead, newer communities such as Overland Park in Kansas and Lee's Summit in Missouri are the preferred destinations of outmigrating residents. City leaders in Independence do not entertain grandiose notions of extraregional competition. They will be satisfied with modest enhancement of the city's position in the region.

Santa Barbara makes much of its uniqueness. The city's 1989 revision of its general plan makes reference to its "unique desirability as a habitat." Consequently, the city has no official desire to become a more important economic player in the region. Instead, city officials want it to become "a better Santa Barbara." If the city were to exploit its development potential, the likely result would engender such a change in quality of life as to be self-defeating. The risk is not of failing; however, attaining a higher economic plane is not a goal worth pursuing. Santa Barbara, with its penchant for introspection, long ago carved out its niche and is committed to the maintenance of it. In becoming a better Santa Barbara, the city has looked to other places with strong waterfront-based tourist economies, such as Charleston. In addition, Santa Barbara borrows from other growth-management cities such as Boulder and Boca Raton. As the mayor puts it, "small really is better."

Cities with Uncertain Orbits

Beaumont has consciously carved out a fairly limited orbit for itself. Its perceptual horizons extend to proximate small cities and an unincorporated territory known as the Golden Triangle. (The three points of the triangle are Beaumont, Port Arthur, and Orange.) City leaders dismiss nearby Houston, a higher-order city of almost 2 million people, as a potential competitor. In what could be thought of as an example of "big frog in small pond" thinking, the leadership contends that Beaumont's role as the dominant point in the Golden Triangle is perfectly acceptable. Although city leaders continue to talk in terms of a self-contained orbit, Beaumont's economic distress portends an uncertain orbit. Admittedly, Beaumont has looked beyond the Triangle area for ideas. For example, in exploring redevelopment strategies, Beaumont leaders traveled to Lowell for inspiration. However, Lowell was a city to emulate, not one to compete with.

Duluth's and Evansville's city officials might easily be viewed through similar lenses. Officials saw their cities' economic positions slip in the postwar period as the national economy moved from heavy manufacturing to other economic bases. Both Duluth and Evansville, heavily dependent upon their manufacturing origins, felt their positions decline while other cities (the Twin Cities, Indianapolis, and Louisville) gained. While officials in neither city saw their economic rivals as these larger, dominant cities, they did sense that, without active government incentives, their competitive positions could sink even further, an outcome they wanted to avoid. Both cities looked at successes in other cities and attempted to adapt them. For example, Duluth emulated Minneapolis's Skywalk, and Evansville emulated the successful restoration of Pittsburgh's train station by restoring its downtown post office. But neither perceived those cities as competitors.

To do more to stimulate development in Duluth or to strive to make the city a more important regional or national center within its system of cities is not, at this time, on the agenda of city officials, nor is it envisioned as Duluth's destiny. City officials are content to take action and to offer financial incentives to bring back Duluth's economic foundation but not to catapult the city to a higher position. The protection of Duluth's small-town atmosphere is not to be sacrificed to aspirations for growing larger than its historically determined, optimal size.

Evansville officials support development projects not for the purpose of competing with larger cities, nor of emulating them; rather, public financial incentives are offered to developers so that the city can maintain its current economic position and not slip farther in relation to other cities. As officials argue, the purpose for public promotion of economic development projects is to improve the employment and income profiles of the city. No one offered the view that the city ought to challenge other regional cities and become the next Cincinnati or Nashville. Rather, their focus seems to be on not slipping behind, becoming an even more minor player among cities.

Springfield, heavily dependent upon its manufacturing base, feels tremendous pressure from other producers of farm implements and other industrial products. Not only are other cities in Illinois and Indiana competing with it for industry, but the neighboring city of Dayton and its suburbs also provide formidable competition. Although the city would like to recoup its former status (the city's population has declined since 1970), its ongoing fiscal crisis and political conservatism have not allowed for much public investment in development projects. The fear of city officials is that Springfield will slip in its system of cities and rank behind the up-and-coming suburbs of Dayton and out-of-state competitors as well. Competitor cities for Springfield officials appear to be those that fall within the city's traditional economic orbits. As a consequence of the dominant political philosophy of the city, city officials are prepared for Springfield to become a smaller city, a less-important city in its relevant system of cities. Not that they wish the city to move down to a lower rung in its city hierarchy; rather, city officials clearly understand that, by not risking city resources in the development process, the distinct possibility exists that Springfield will descend in the hierarchy of its relevant system of cities.

CONCLUDING OBSERVATIONS

Perceptual orbits frequently (but not universally) define a different set of relevant cities than standard economic orbits. If city officials believe they are competing with cities on a different plane, they might be persuaded to mobilize different development tools than if they perceive their competitors as similarly situated cities. If these cities constitute the officials' vision of an ideal city, then these officials might make investments for purposes of emulating these other cities. This may (or may not) result in the desired alteration of their own city's real economic orbit. Politics matters in mapping out these new orbits, because local officials perceive a relevant orbit and then try to mobilize public capital in a manner that moves the city to a newly defined level. These perceptual orbits may indeed be the forces that integrate public capital mobilization and urban outcomes (or images of the good society)—a theme we develop in chapter 6.

3 / ASPIRATIONS, VISIONS, AND IMAGES

LEWIS MUMFORD defines the city as "the point of maximum concentration for the power and culture of a community."[1] The city does not simply happen, rather "the city . . . is a cumulative product, the creation of many lifetimes of creative effort."[2] Local government leaders have aspirations for their city: they aspire to maintain or change their city's competitive position or rank within the relevant system of cities. As the possessors of public authority in the community, city officials take actions they believe will achieve this objective. A city's financial health depends on any number of factors, and important among them are these aspirations of local leaders. Frequently, discussions of aspirations are couched in terms of the city's image, which can be translated into action because of local authority.

THE CONCEPT OF IMAGE

City building, at its very core an activity involving capital investment and land use, is also very importantly an effort at image creation or preservation. Admittedly, the effort and energy expended in pursuit of image varies from one city to another and, within a city, from one period to another. In general, however, the development history of U.S. cities is one of striving toward an idealized state, of aiming for a representation of reality.

Image is an interesting concept. Dictionary definitions underscore its duality: it refers to a concept of someone or something held by the public and also to the character projected by someone or something to the public. In other words, image is both perceived and projected. Kenneth Boulding defines image as "subjective knowledge."[3] Here, the focus is upon public image—the shared images of many individuals. Those images are mental representations, often expressed as impressions, ideas, and metaphors. A 1971 issue of *Public Interest* contains two substantively different articles, one entitled "The City as Sandbox," the other "The City as Reservation," each of which evokes a central, if not unsettling, mental image of America's central cities.[4]

Urban sociologists have looked at the city microscopically and macroscopically, with evaluations both positive and negative. Four general images of the city have resulted: the city as bazaar, the city as jungle, the city as organism, and the city as machine.[5] The city as bazaar, a positive, microscopic image, envisions the city as a place of diversity and activity. A visitor from the countryside is astounded by the array of experiences and opportunities available in this captivating smorgasbord. This positive image is counterbalanced by a negative one, that of the city as jungle, its activity and diversity representing density and danger, the city as a place of chaos, competition, and fear. A positive, macroscopic image is conveyed in the city as organism, which sees the city as a highly specialized, interacting system. Interrelated parts create the community and serve the common good. The city as machine, however, offers a more negative image. Lost is any sense of the benign guidance of the organism. Instead, the city is controlled by business, political, and professional elites, who serve their own interests with little concern for the common welfare.

These scholarly images may or may not correspond with popular images of cities. Rosellen Brown muses, "think of certain cities and you see the flash and shapely flow of water. No one would have trouble identifying them solely by the configuration of buildings on the banks of their rivers—the Thames, the Seine, the Danube . . . . Lodged almost as firmly in the collective mind are the drastically inland places—Phoenix, Denver." And, "most people's image of Houston is, in fact, an odd amalgam of Hollywood Old West—the hot, dry, desert of cowboy heroes—and tall canyons of glass monoliths, hard-edged skyscrapers a dozen deep, reflecting back the empty sky of Texas."[6]

Cities' images are not the same all of the time and are not the same to all people. Conflicting impressions and contradictory images exist. George Perry speaks of the "endless contradictions" that are Baltimore.[7] Images, therefore, are dynamic and cannot be separated from the context of the evaluator (or viewer). Kevin Lynch argues both dynamism and context: "Not only is the city an object which is perceived (and perhaps enjoyed) by millions of people of widely diverse class and character, but it is the product of many builders who are constantly modifying the structure for reasons of their own. While it may be stable in general outlines for some time, it is ever changing in detail. Only partial control can be exercised over its growth and form. There is no final result, only a continuous succession of phases. . . . The image of the Manhattan skyline may stand for vitality, power, decadence, mystery, congestion, greatness, or what you will, but in each case that sharp picture crystallizes and reinforces the meaning."[8]

Cities are so complex and multifaceted that understanding them requires a certain degree of reductionism. "The city, as a whole, is inaccessible to the imagination unless it can be reduced and simplified."[9] Thus is the magic of image, which opens a world far beyond our experience. The media, of course, play a major role in this process. When the Minnesota Twins squared off against the Atlanta Braves in the 1991 World Series, a *New York Times* sportswriter summoned up these images: "It's the city of Giants in the Earth, Prince and Garrison Keillor against the city of Scarlett and black political power and CNN."[10] In Detroit, local officials lament the media treatment accorded the city as "Detroit bashing." They point to a summer 1990 *New York Times Magazine* article entitled "The Tragedy of Detroit" as indicative of the city's bad press, although certainly the 1967 riots didn't help its image.[11]

There is a tendency to speak of a city adjectivally.[12] But images of a city are not immutable; they evolve. For example, Miami and Los Angeles, cities "built on the power of dreamscape, collective fantasy, and facade," have undergone a series of transformations in the twentieth century.[13] Miami, once an enclave like Palm Beach, has become a multiethnic microcosm of global exchange. It functions in an expanded system of cities and has a different image. "It is now the happening capital of the Caribbean, soaked in drug money and a setting for stylish cop shows."[14] Los Angeles, created as production space for the film industry, has decentralized and recentralized in response to demographic and economic shifts. Its image is almost mythical. "Mellow, laid-back, casual, ever-richer, far-out, unhurried L.A., drenched in nearly constant sun, festooned with exotic palm trees, populated by the beautiful and the celebrated, edged by miles of beach."[15]

In transforming aspirations and visions into reality, local officials attempt to project a favorable and distinct image of the city. One approach to image projection is the creation of a unique place identity, a symbol so prominent that it *is* the city.[16] The Empire State Building, Wall Street, and Times Square have come to symbolize New York City, while the Sears Tower and Wrigley Field have done the same for Chicago. The Washington Monument means Washington, D.C., the Arch means St. Louis, the Space Needle means Seattle, the Astrodome means Houston. These readily identifiable landmarks are unique, peculiar to a specific place, and are seldom mistaken.

Emphasizing and cultivating place-specific differences is particularly appealing to second-tier cities that have not traditionally enjoyed locational or positional advantages. Chattanooga, for example, opened the world's largest freshwater aquarium in 1992 in an effort at municipal specialness. (Many cities, notably Baltimore, Monterey, and New Orleans, have aquariums, but they typically feature saltwater exhibits.) Many cities package and market their own particular qualities and traits in an effort to gain a competitive advantage. Cities are recognizing their "endogenous potentials" and are carving out unique profiles.[17] A newly differentiated urban hierarchy is the result. Thus a city such as San Jose, which is part of the San Francisco constellation, has little interest in emulating its famous neighbor to the north. Instead San Jose is emerging as a differentiated star, with its own identity.

Opponents of a proposal for a $400-million gambling casino in downtown New Orleans feared a loss of place-specific identity. They consciously traded in images in their unsuccessful attempts to derail the plan. Positive reinforcing images of "the city's distinctive French Creole character" and "its graceful old architecture" were summoned up. The casino, it was argued, would "transform city streets into a Las Vegas or an Atlantic City," images designed to evoke negative reactions.[18] Opponents did not want to see New Orleans compete in a system of cities defined by casino gambling.

Image creation is central to economic development strategies, especially in cities that aspire to a higher level. Leaders of the local Chamber of Commerce in Columbia, South Carolina, had a surprise in store when they set out to discover what people in other parts of the country thought about the city. "We heard everything from, 'It's a country in South America,' to 'Isn't that the next space shuttle?' It wasn't that Columbia had a bad image, it just didn't have an image."[19] This was unwelcome news to a city in which the chamber was in the midst of a four-year, $2.2-million economic development drive. As a consequence, city leaders launched an image-building campaign with the slogan We're Growing Proud. Discouraged when that slogan failed to inspire, the city adopted a new one in 1993. Building on its status as the seat of state government, the slogan became Columbia: A Capital Place to Be.

IMAGES AND ECONOMIC DEVELOPMENT

Cities are concerned about their images. City leaders, as a group, share a collective vision of what the city could, or should, become. In pursuit of this vision, cities mobilize public capital. The effects of public action, then, can be measured in more ways than simply return on investment. Cities sometimes give away public resources for reasons other than generating financial reward or return on investment.[20] They do this in an effort to move the city toward an aspired end state. Classical literature is full of these end states: the Platonic and Aristotelian images of the polis, Augustine's City of God, or the more contemporary City Beautiful of Daniel Burnham and his followers. But to move beyond the plans laid out in Ebenezer Howard's *Garden Cities of To-morrow* or Le Corbusier's towering Radiant City to actually implement some of the recommendations requires government action or collaboration. In the two decades following the publication of Burnham's *Plan of Chicago,* the city of Chicago spent $300 million on its suggested improvements.[21] More recently, $30 million in public money went into Columbus, Ohio's, Ameriflora '92, an international flower show to commemorate the quincentennial of the city's namesake's landing in the New World. The intent was simple—to create a positive, upbeat, and yes, beautiful image of Ohio's largest city. As one resident put it, "We're kind of a forgotten city."[22] Ameriflora, with one-third of its costs underwritten by government, was expected to make Columbus more visible in the collective mind of the nation. The purpose of such public action is to portray a dynamic and evolving image of the city.

Images can take the form of economic development goals for a city. City leaders have a vision for their city, and economic development is a large part of that vision. Development projects, be they industrial or commercial, are often promoted because they will provide jobs and generate revenues that benefit the city. But just as important, these projects are tangible symbols of survival, transformation, or ascendance, depending on the city's circumstances. In fact, depending on how the deal is structured, on the degree of risk, and on the intentions of local officials, symbolic value may be the sole return that a city gets from a project.

This is not to suggest that economic development is necessarily a consensus issue in American communities. Paul Peterson's catalytic argument—that cities must pursue development policy to survive—structured much of the debate in the urban politics literature in the 1980s.[23] Throughout the period, city leaders took public support of economic development projects as a given. Under the banner of job creation and downtown revitalization, public dollars underwrote development projects around the country. The public rallied around the economic development flag. Citizen support, or perhaps acquiescence, could be easily attained. Economic development was conceived as a competitive venture, a means of keeping up with or getting ahead of, other cities.

Scholars and citizens have begun to question the emphasis on economic development. A headline in the *Charlotte Observer* sums up the issue: "World-Class City? Some Voters Say, So What?"[24] "As Charlotte's national stature grows," says the article, "so does the discontent among ordinary people right here in the neighborhood." Ironically, this discontent occurred at a time when the city was being portrayed by national news media as "a prime-time player in the New South boom. But increasingly," the article continues, "voters wonder if elected officials are too concerned about image—tall buildings and convention centers—and less concerned about other, more basic needs." Charlotte had allocated $15 million for a performing arts center, $35 million for land for an NFL stadium, and $150 million for a new convention center. The article quotes a resident as wondering if city officials were "more influenced by being a world-class city than they should be . . . it's all right to be ambitious for the city, but . . ."[25] Another resident asked, "Who are we trying to catch?" Charlotte's effort to move up, and to use public dollars to do so, is not unusual. San Antonio Mayor Henry Cisneros's last hurrah as he left office was to convince a majority of citizens that, without a major league ballpark, San Antonio could never be a major league city. Amid skepticism, a sales tax was passed by the electorate to finance construction of the dome. *World class* and *major league* are labels that matter to city officials in Charlotte and San Antonio and in many other cities as well.

IMAGE CREATION

Image, then, is not only an abstraction, it is a guide for purposive action by local officials. Whether this action reflects the business community's needs and influence or whether it represents class conflict is beyond the scope of this book. Only local officials have the legal authority to sign the deals and carry out the plans. Local officials, as repositories of a city's vision and as shapers of that vision, engage in development. Consequently, that vision is dynamic. As the power structure changes or regimes shift, the image of the city also shifts, reflecting the new political alignment. As vision or image changes, so does the city's economic development function. It becomes more active, more diversified, more aggressive, or it becomes less so, as has been demonstrated in the growth management movement.

Semiotics, the study of signs, offers a way to understand city image.[26] Signs are composed of a signifier (a set of elements that provide meaning) and a signified (a message derived from the signifier by an observer). The signifier and the signified may not jibe; that is, the meaning and the message may not coincide. A city park with green space, fountains, and benches may have been constructed to convey a specific image of the community, perhaps one of serenity. To passersby and park users, the message may be quite different—"a waste of tax dollars," "a place to play," "beautiful scenery," "a temporary home." Quite simply, "meaning in the city is multi-coded."[27] Connotations differ from denotations, and both may change over time. A vacant office tower, once a source of employment and production and signifying prosperity and power, is a source of emptiness and vandalism and now signifies failure and hopelessness. The image of the city is a symbolic complex and a symbolic system. It is a sign. "There is no image without an affective resonance."[28]

According to M. Gottdiener, "the most important collective representation in the battle between cities for resources is that projected by growth coalitions—the specific combination of public and private interests promoting the development of the city. These are images produced and managed by city interests and for use in specific forums . . . they are not fixed images but vary according to the audience they are intended to reach or the message they are asked to convey." Farther on, he notes that "the urban image must be read as ideology, as an historical product, as a gesture with a past, as an outcome of a class society propelled by powerful forces of development and change."[29] The city is, indisputably, a place of contending interests. Growth-machine interests have been successful, either through domination or persuasion, in establishing their image as the consensus image, or what Gerald Suttles calls the "collective representation" of the city.[30] We contend that a positive and attractive image is one of the tools a city can use to lure investors. Nevertheless, the battle to establish what Gottdiener labels "symbolic hegemony" is ongoing. Gottdiener, who is critical of the work of urban ecologists, is correct when he argues that symbolic appeals alone rarely play a determining role in the competition for resources. It is accurate to see image as a "conjunctural mediator" that works with other, nonsymbolic factors.

Acknowledging that images have social contexts and that other factors affect investment decisions does not vitiate our argument. It is true that below the surface of the city are contentious groups struggling over alternate signs. In economic development, it is the vision of the regime that generally prevails. Local officials who negotiate with developers and other business interests ultimately decide which development tools to provide for the purpose of approximating their collective vision of what the city can become. Our assumption, then, is that the behavior and development decisions of top city officials approximate their subjective interpretation of where the city ought to be heading. Harold Wolman, in a study on city mayors' "mental maps," argues similarly: "The mental maps of local political elites are related to elite behavior."[31]

THE STUDY CITIES AND THEIR IMAGES

The list below and the discussion that follows summarize the images and the visions for the future for the 10 case study cities, synthesized from 1988 and 1989 interviews and written perspectives of top city leaders. These images are dynamic and therefore may not accurately describe the city's image today—a point we take up again in chapter 7.

- *Cities with expanding orbits*
  Boise
    Image: Isolated potato town
    Vision: Rocky Mountain entrepreneurial leader
  Huntsville
    Image: Old South cotton, defense
    Vision: Booming New South, high technology

Lowell
  Image: Revitalized mill town
  Vision: Preeminent middle-sized city
Orlando
  Image: Sun, Mickey Mouse, tourism
  Vision: World-class primate city

- *Cities with self-contained orbits*
Independence
  Image: Blue-collar suburb
  Vision: Independent, full-service, second-tier city
Santa Barbara
  Image: Stylish resort community
  Vision: Unique refuge from the commonplace

- *Cities with uncertain orbits*
Beaumont
  Image: Dirty industrial town
  Vision: Regional cultural mecca
Duluth
  Image: Cold industrial outpost
  Vision: Economically diverse regional town
Evansville
  Image: Declining industrial river town
  Vision: Vibrant industrial river town
Springfield
  Image: Declining industrial town
  Vision: Stable industrial town

Boise

Into the 1980s, Boise had an image problem. It was the leading city in a decidedly nonleading state. While Boise may have been the economic and political center of Idaho, the most widely held image of the state involved potatoes. (The Famous Potatoes slogan on Idaho's license plates was effective.) And Boise itself, characterized by a conservative (some refer to it as somnolent) leadership, did little to present a more dynamic, Boise-specific image to the outside world.

All of this changed in the mid-1980s, when Boise experienced a regime shift. Voters replaced the existing leadership with substantially more proactive officials. A new vision of the city is one of the most obvious results. The mayor's 1987–88 budget message used phrases such as "first steps in a new direction" and "building the foundation of a new future." Boise is increasingly less satisfied to be just the dominant city in Idaho. Instead, talk is of moving toward a regional prominence.

The issue of leadership is pivotal in Boise, given its government structure. By the late 1980s, development officials were extolling the new coalition, referring to its leader as "the right mayor at the right time." This new team reoriented local thinking away from its 20-year deadlock over the choice of downtown renewal *or* a regional mall toward downtown renewal *and* a regional mall. The elements were there, but it took a new regime to push the city off dead center. The current crop of Boise leaders displays not only an awareness of other cities' actions and innovations but a willingness to emulate them.

Several informants in Boise suggested that the city is wrestling with its vision. Boise had been a quintessential risk-averse city in earlier periods. Fiscal conservatism and a slow-growth philosophy effectively kept Boise under wraps. That has changed, but the city is not yet quite comfortable with its grandiose vision. The orientation is toward the future, and the vision of the future is upbeat, filled with optimism, with Boise as the bold new city of the Rocky Mountain West—and beyond. Generally, Boise leaders see their city as undiscovered and their role as one of simply tapping and directing its potential. In response to the question, How will they know when they have been successful? the answer is quite simple: when other cities look to Boise as an example of creativity and innovation. And those other cities are not Spokane or even Salt Lake City. Local leaders note with pride that when locally headquartered Micron Technologies was considering expansion, it considered moving to cities such as Portland, Phoenix, and Kansas City before deciding to expand in Boise.

Huntsville

On the whole, Huntsville's leaders exhibit a bit of discomfiture about being in Alabama. According to well-placed Huntsvillians, the image of the state of Alabama acts as a ball and chain on the city. And the state is not particularly enthralled about Huntsville. The prevailing attitude among Alabama politicians is resentment toward the Yankees in Huntsville and the easy money (read, federal dollars) that Huntsville has enjoyed. For its part, Huntsville has long felt somewhat estranged from the state. The city is a scant 15 miles from the Tennessee state line, far closer than to Montgomery, Alabama's capital, or Birmingham, Alabama's largest city. The city's challenge has been to pursue a decidedly non-Alabamian image. Thus cottonfields made way for space-age industry. As one local notable commented, this makes for "interesting community dynamics . . . Huntsville has the old landed gentry and new high-tech entrepreneurship amid Southern redneck culture."

Huntsville's regime wants people to think of Huntsville in terms of glittering, powerful images. Rockets blasting into the sky, lasers piercing the air, computers digesting huge amounts of electronic data, satellite dishes scanning the stars, robots assembling complicated electrical devices in the sparkling clean "safe" environments of the city's industries. These images are, of course, decidedly "high tech." The city's leaders intend to continue to capitalize on advanced research, development, and marketing activities. They like to say that "the future is our business in Huntsville." Figure 3.1 shows how Huntsville markets itself as a limitless place, as a community reaching for the stars. The Chamber of Commerce has adopted the rocket logo and The Sky Is Not the Limit slogan to convey the possibilities.

In Huntsville, there are no reservations about using the public sector to prime the economic development pump. The "old money" interests reaped a tremendous benefit when their land values skyrocketed after the federal government located defense installations in and around the city. They saw what federal spending meant to the community. It was a compelling lesson. And they recognized the value of government infrastructure. Since the late 1960s, there has emerged a new technocratic wealth. These "new money" individuals are moving beyond business and into community politics. For example, the mayor elected in 1989 is an engineer who had come to town to work on the Saturn project.

The city has formalized its aspirations in Vision 2000, a plan for the city's economic stability and opportunity. For Huntsville, a healthy economy involves partnerships between private and public interests. There is general consensus among the leadership that the private sector's role is initiation and risk, the public sector's is one of infrastructure development. The Vision 2000 report acknowledges fierce intercity competition, and it is clear that Huntsville does not intend to be at a comparative disadvantage. Currently, the city is nurturing an Atlanta-to-Memphis high-technology corridor, with Huntsville firmly at its center. Huntsville looks to San Jose and Boston as areas of comparison.

Figure 3.1 Huntsville Logo Inspired by the Space Industry. Used with permission of the Chamber of Commerce of Huntsville/Madison County.

Local leaders flatly state that Huntsville will definitely eclipse Birmingham and become a major regional city. The four crucial elements in this scenario are the airport, local universities, infrastructure improvements, and the city's positive image. The mayor has a 10-year, $200-million capital improvements plan, with half of the money allocated for transportation. (When the interstate highway system was designed, Huntsville was one of the small towns left out. Now, it is one of the largest cities in the country without an interstate spur, a condition that is being corrected.) Much of the remaining funds will go to quality-of-life variables, such as buying 540 acres of mountainside and supporting the development of the arts, sports, and museums. Huntsville's motto could easily be You've Got to Spend Money to Make Money.

Lowell

The city government's vision of Lowell is probably best described in the Lowell Plan: Lowell wants to be the "preeminent middle-sized city in America." Civic leaders believe that the city's strengths lie in its past, which should be turned into an asset. The canals, which have not been used in decades, the abandoned and decaying textile mills, the old housing and close-knit neighborhoods all must be preserved and function as the foundation for the city's future. The city has learned not to "put all its eggs in one basket," according to a former planning and development director, meaning, of course, that Lowell should not rely on one industry for sustenance (as it did in the past with the textile industry). Diversification of the city's and the region's economic bases will augur much better for the future than a one-industry economic base could ever have done.

The Lowell Plan, Inc., and city officials view the Lowell of the future as a city of approximately 100,000 population, a clean, middle-sized city, an alternative to the cramped and crowded Boston, a progressive, high-technology city that can work with investors and developers. Although heavy manufacturing has not been forsaken, neither does it rate high on the kinds of industries and workforce city officials want to attract. The blue-collar, industrial textile town is gone forever, preserved only in the pages of history books and in the Lowell National Historical Park. The planning and development director contends that Lowell did not develop its vision on the basis of a successful model elsewhere; the city does not emulate any other city, nor does it want to. Its vision of the future is strictly homegrown. Leaders of other cities, however, from both the United States and around the world, travel to Lowell for the express purpose of learning from its successes. According to the *Wall Street Journal, Newsweek,* and other publications, Lowell in the early to mid-1980s was the national benchmark for successful development and particularly for successful public-private cooperation to foster development.[32]

But the vision that seems to have gained credence among observers across the nation only partially reflects reality. What city officials say and what city officials do are strangely unrelated; it is almost as if the economic nightmare of the past century still haunts city officials' every move. Two important contradictions are worth pursuing.

The first is the presumed lessons of dependence on one industry, textiles. Although Lowellians readily admit the fallacy of heavy reliance on one industry, there appears to be little that indicates the lesson transcends the textile industry or heavy manufacturing. As Patricia Flynn of the Federal Reserve notes, in the early nineteenth century the textile industry was considered high technology, but that has changed. Now high technology means accounting, office, and computers. By 1982 this modern-day high-technology industry "accounted for 40 percent of all manufacturing employment in the Lowell area."[33] Her fear, or guarded pessimism, about the permanence of Lowell's economic turnaround is premised on an analysis of product life cycles, namely, that as high-technology industries mature and shift to standardized production processes, they relocate to lower-cost cities and nations. Lowell, because of its economic miracle of the past decade, is not one of those low-cost areas. Hence, Lowell needs to diversify further.

The second, and certainly more important, contradiction is the future view of Lowell. City officials want Lowell to be the preeminent middle-sized city. City officials seem to think that a population of 100,000 or 115,000 is ideal. An observer might deduce that once the city reaches that optimal size, it would use its control of public financing tools to manage or reduce or even halt its economic growth. Contrary to logic, however, the city continues to promote its development program at a frenzied pace. City officials and private investors are not content with recovering the lost ground of this century and holding the line on growth. Rather, even as late as the mid-1980s, there was a concerted effort to move Lowell up to a higher economic rung in relation to relevant cities. City officials and private investors, especially the city's (public and private) movers and shakers on the board of directors of the Lowell Plan, Inc., aspire to make Lowell a more important economic actor than it ever was in the past and certainly more dominant within its relevant system of cities than pronouncements like "preeminent middle-sized city" might suggest for the future.

Orlando

Of all the study cities, no city officials exuded more confidence about a city's future nor brimmed over with more optimism about the permanence of the booming economy than Orlando's. Their vision of the city's future can be likened to the futuristic visions of the City Beautiful school. City parks surrounding beautiful lakes, elegant buildings attractive to tourists and shoppers, broad boulevards and highways wending their ways through the sprawling city, clusters of smaller commercial establishments scattered throughout the broad city, a city of glass and concrete and green spaces. The aspirations and actions of city officials in promoting this futuristic vision spring from the nearly uninterrupted, two-decade-long era of economic growth and the magnetic tourist appeal of the larger metropolitan area.

In promoting the city, city officials are informed by two perspectives. The first is the fear that Walt Disney World, which lies outside the city of Orlando, will overtake Orlando in retail trade, commerce, and other business activity. The city, therefore, actively promotes its downtown area and neighborhood retail sections of the city—what one official called Orlando's "urban villages." The second perspective is that, to attract investment, the city has become very design conscious. Attractive public areas around the city's many lakes, major landscaping projects in the downtown areas, and architectural design requirements for the first three floors of new or renovated buildings in the downtown core all reflect the vision of city leaders to become a "world-class city."

City leaders believe that Orlando's image compares favorably with those of much larger cities, such as Phoenix, Atlanta, San Diego, and Charlotte. Indeed, probably the most ironic aspect of city leaders' vision for Orlando is that none of those cities has been as small as Orlando for decades. With fewer than 200,000 year-round residents, Orlando might seem to be out of its league against these and other larger cities—even those within the state. But Orlando officials do not view Jacksonville, Miami, or even rapidly growing Tampa as cities they want to emulate.[34] Rather, as several top city officials put it, Orlando wants to be a world-class city. Their proof: no other city of similar size can boast a National Basketball Association team. Their vision of Orlando and its future hinges on diversifying the already rapidly growing economic base (high-technology industries in particular) and on strengthening the neighborhoods to be urban villages.

Independence

In the mid–nineteenth century, Independence was a jumping-off point for westward expansion. In the closing days of the twentieth century, the city is struggling with its image. For the most part, Independence is perceived as a residential suburb of Kansas City. Figures on the number of workers who leave Independence each morning for jobs in Kansas City support that perception. In addition, Independence is considered a bit shopworn, unlike the crisp new suburbs surrounding it. But Independence has a long history, which, short of the Conestoga wagon on its official seal, it has been slow to capitalize on, to weave into its identity. The fact that Independence is even the least familiar to Americans over the age of 40 is because it was the home of President Harry Truman.

Like most metropolitan areas, the Kansas City area is experiencing a steady decentralization of economic activity. And like other communities adjacent to Kansas City, Independence hopes to capture some of that relocating enterprise. It counts its quality of life, good environment, and low crime rate among its attributes. Greater commercial and industrial investment will allow Independence to achieve one of its other goals: local jobs for its residents. The desire that Independence become something more than a bedroom community ("a city in its own right," is the way one elected official phrased it) is fairly consistent among city leaders. However, there is substantial disagreement as to whether the city should alter its image and adopt a more vigorous development-promoting orientation. One camp supports the creation of a new, more vibrant image for Independence and more government-assisted development. The other favors the maintenance of Independence's traditional small-town identity and a minimalist role for government in development. Consequently, despite the appearance of tranquility, politics in Independence can be quite volatile.

In the late 1980s, the city hit upon tourism as an economic development strategy. A 1989 tourism study states "it has become obvious that both the real and perceived perceptions concerning the physical image of the City need to be improved."[35] The study went on to recommend city beautification, signage improvements, and continuity in presentation as activities that could lead to image enhancement. The Truman home, which is operated by the National Park Servce, and the Truman library and museum, which is managed by the National Archives, would continue to be the hub of the tourism effort. In addition, a state-owned, city-operated National Frontier Trails Center, celebrating Independence's role in westward expansion, was scheduled for completion in the early 1990s.

Although Independence's population more than doubled between 1950 and 1970, the growth rate has remained relatively flat since 1970. The city's inability to attract a substantial portion of upscale residential and commercial development is attributed to its image and to the existence of more desirable communities in the metropolitan area, especially across the Missouri River in Kansas. In the view of Independence officials, communities such as Overland Park, Kansas, operate at a comparative advantage because the state of Kansas makes it easier for development to occur. Politically conservative Missouri, where referendums are required on local tax and fee increases, creates obstacles for revenue-hungry Independence.

As noted above, despite pronouncements of change and redirection, there is considerable sentiment militating against a larger pump-priming role for city government. Some of the confusion about the city's direction reflects lack of consensus among city leaders. In the 1980s, the city council was strongly factionalized. (For example, two council members mounted a recall effort against the mayor. The mayor survived the recall election, but council squabbling continues.) The city council is seldom of one mind regarding the city's future. While one group of council members talked of an aggressive image-altering development plan, others balked, extolling the small-town nature of Independence and its solid blue-collar base. The latter faction, referred to in the local press as the Dixiecrat coalition, has typically opposed incentives for business. The development-oriented faction, composed primarily of moderate Republicans, has been unable to gain enough adherents to break the gridlock. Consequently, a proposed office park and golf course, a joint venture of the city and private investors, stalled because of funding problems and official malaise.

The prodevelopment faction on the council has high hopes for an area of the city called the Little Blue River Valley. There, the Army Corps of Engineers is completing a project that will take the land out of the 100-year floodplain, thus making it suitable for development. Yet with voters fairly consistently rejecting bond issues and a risk-averse financial community, development is likely to proceed slowly. Whether Independence will effect an image transformation or remain Independence as usual is the issue of the 1990s.

Santa Barbara

The aspiration in Santa Barbara is to become a "better" Santa Barbara. The city has long used the slogan A Refuge from the Commonplace to signify its vision. Santa Barbara has a comparative advantage over many other communities: developers avidly seek entry to the market. However, city leaders realize that no water, snarled traffic, and bad air will take the bloom off the Santa Barbara bougainvillea. To become a better Santa Barbara, the city must live within its resources. Resource balance is not simply the latest California fad; the challenge for Santa Barbara is to do it. In the late 1980s, the city updated its general plan to reflect the growing concern over resource balance. It is in this document that the city's vision is given life.

The concern structuring decisionmaking in Santa Barbara is its quality of life. In the development realm, the key variable is whether a project is compatible with the Santa Barbara image. This vision has evolved from an earlier, much more common, development goal. A history of Santa Barbara documents the city's repeated efforts to exploit the commercial potential of its harbor. Why? "A desire to become Southern California's most successful community was at the heart of the harbor debate."[36] Times have changed, and this vision has been supplanted; now success is defined quite differently.

The city's vision is captured in its struggle with the growth question. In 1975, after an extensive study of the impacts of growth, the city's population goal was changed from 140,000 to 85,000. The city restricted the number of residential units, but the council did not deal with the industrial and commercial aspects of growth. The city charter was amended in 1982 to mandate resource balance in the city's development policies. After five years of technical studies on water, traffic, housing, and economics, the city, in 1988, began updating its general plan and addressing issues of nonresidential growth so as to become a self-sufficient city. Santa Barbara considers itself a national leader in confronting issues of resource balance.

In updating the general plan, city government raised three fundamental questions: How much development should be allowed? What type of economic opportunities should be emphasized? Will development alter the character of the city? Several alternatives were posited, ranging from a virtual moratorium on development to the full development of commercial zones. Thus in 1988 and 1989, city leaders and the public wrestled with reconciling the consensual goals of living within resources, ensuring a strong economy, and maintaining Santa Barbara's "unique desirability."

Beaumont

Beaumont, one of the most highly industrialized communities in Texas, has a reputation as, in the words of one city leader, "a dirty industrial city with a blue-collar mentality." Beaumont evinces little interest in competing with or modeling itself after higher-order cities. In fact, Beaumont officials are fond of saying that their city could have been what Houston has become, that Beaumont was more advantageously situated (both geographically and economically) to become the dominant city in the region. Instead, key leaders (both public and private sectors) consciously pursued a strategy of control, especially insofar as development initiatives from the outside were concerned. The aspiration in Beaumont is to remain the major city in what is referred to as the Golden Triangle—the surrounding industrial area, consisting of smaller cities and unincorporated territory. No visions of Tulsa or New Orleans, relatively proximate cities that might possibly serve as models, dance in the heads of city officials.

The collective weight of these orientations and conditions effectively restricts the mobilization of public capital. Beaumont is a risk-averse community. Even if a philosophical shift were to occur, the harsh reality of the oil bust and the memory of an investment mistake that cost the city $4 million would quickly discredit any risk-laden ventures. City officials claim that it would be hard to overstate the impact of the investment scandal, coming as it did on the heels of the oil industry's problems. After that, as one official put it, "no one trusted the city." Beaumont officials are willing to engage in activities such as rezoning and sponsorship of primarily symbolic "economic summits." The first summit invited the public to join the "world's largest economic development committee"; the second focused on community organizations; the third targeted small businesses. (City officials readily acknowledge the pep rally nature of the summits. Their intent is to reverse the negative citizen attitude about the community.) Beaumont wields its power of eminent domain fairly cautiously. This is a city in which the phrases "public purpose" and "public need" are fighting words. The city has begun modest attempts at stimulating diversification of the local economy, all the while hoping that market forces will hasten recovery.

The city's 1986 annual report, distributed in the wake of the investment scandal, notes that Beaumont is like a mountain climber halfway to the top, "poised to either move upward or to edge back down." Given that precarious position, the city government is making incremental moves designed to advance Beaumont upward. But even if their efforts are unsuccessful, little of fundamental value will have been risked. Beaumont uses development tools sparingly. One explanation lies in the relative newness of many of the state-sponsored initiatives; comparative state research seldom finds Texas a leading innovator in public policy. This tendency plus a vibrant economy in the 1970s meant that Texas came late to development-promoting policy. The troubled economic climate of the early 1980s pushed the state government into action, and the state began to make available to local governments tax-increment financing districts and enterprise zones.[37]

It is the downtown area of the city that has come in for special attention. Beaumont's vision was physically altered when a consultant's report encouraged the city to reorient downtown, toward the river. Riverfront Park was one result. Later, in the mid-1980s, a study prepared for the Economic Development Administration advocated an economic reorientation of downtown away from shopping and commerce and toward government and culture. The city took the study to heart and supports a number of ventures intended to achieve that objective, such as using a series of land swaps to relocate the Southeast Texas Art Museum to the downtown area. The emerging vision is of Beaumont as a cultural mecca, with the city government's role primarily exhortation. One visible challenge facing the city is the LaSalle Hotel property, located a block from City Hall. The building, a luxury hotel of a bygone era, has become extremely dilapidated. Its hulking presence overshadows everything that the city is trying to do in the downtown area.

Duluth

Geographically, Duluth is a fairly isolated, medium-sized city. Only Minneapolis and St. Paul, a short two- to three-hour drive to the south, provide any close referent points. Competition with similar-sized and similarly situated cities, consequently, is not perceived by local officials in concrete terms. City officials can identify development projects from other cities as cutting edge and worthy of emulation, but they reject any implication that their city is competing with another city. Nevertheless, they did express a vision of their city, a direction of where they wanted it to go, a dream, a set of goals and aspirations. This vision is simultaneously nostalgic and forward looking, an uncanny reification of the theme from the movie *Back to the Future.*

Duluth, argue city officials and key observers, experienced its economic and demographic zenith decades ago. The future city, according to official city pronouncements and all city officials interviewed for this study, should be similar in size to the city of the past. But city officials hasten to add that its economic foundation should not reflect the past. Total reliance on heavy manufacturing is not the vision they hold for Duluth; rather, the future city must encourage diversification of its economic base (e.g., tourism, medical care) and promote its physical attractiveness.

Nor are their aspirations rooted in a need to emulate medium-sized, high-technology growth centers. Duluth is not situated geographically, nor in terms of proximity to institutes of higher education (like Silicon Valley in California, Route 128 near Boston), to take advantage of growth in the high-technology sector. Duluthians believe, instead, that the city should capitalize on at least three of its four identified strengths, defined by city officials as a tourist center, a medical facilities center, and a retail trade center (they also identified education, but weren't convinced of their successes in this arena). This approach to capitalizing on three of their four key assets would establish Duluth as a regional hub of northern

Minnesota, northern Wisconsin, and the Upper Peninsula of Michigan. Further, should the city be successful in capitalizing on those strengths, it would result in population growth that should ebb at the levels of several decades ago, near 100,000 or slightly greater. For example, one Duluthian averred that "the city's vision is completely internal; there is no emulation of any similar or competing city. It looks to Baltimore's and Toledo's successful harbor projects, but not to those cities for emulation." A city planner echoed the same refrain: "[Duluth] is trying to develop a new 'image.' If the city puts on a more confident image, then it might encourage [further private] investment in the city." The planning and development director conceded that "Duluth competes most directly with Minneapolis–St. Paul, [but] we don't want to be like Minneapolis–St. Paul." That is to say, Duluthians like the small-town environment.

To protect its small-town, intimate atmosphere (one city official labeled it "romantic"), city officials have recently become a smidgen more cautious, a bit more risk averse in their public offerings for development, compared to the early 1980s. During that time, the city was prepared to accommodate nearly any project if it had even a remote possibility of stimulating development. City officials fear that too much public assistance for development, resulting in successful projects, might push Duluth beyond some optimal point. That point is called the New Duluth of the Past, a vibrant, economically diversified, regional hub city of 100,000. With the perceived successes of symbolically important development projects, these city officials are now reconsidering the breadth of public financial assistance for development.

The pessimism of the 1970s, that Duluth might join company with many sunken ore ships in Lake Superior, has given way to a vision of a bright future, one that includes a much more dynamic, diverse, and buoyant economy but that also reflects Duluthians' desire to resurrect the glorious past and revive the quality of life from that era.

Evansville

Tucked away in the hills of southwestern Indiana, Evansville has always been a relatively small city. Residents think of themselves as citizens of a small town, and a quaint provincialism prevails. In conversation, city officials reflect this isolation in their views of the city's future. Evansville, they insist, will never be a large city, nor should it try to become one. In fact, Evansville should never be much larger than it is now, nor should it finance public development programs that might operate with that assumption in mind.

Moreover, Evansville officials do not want their city to become competitive with other regional cities, such as Louisville or Nashville, nor do they wish to emulate those cities. Rather, development finance incentives employed elsewhere are studied for their applicability to Evansville. For example, refurbishing a turn-of-the-century post office and developing boutique shops and restaurants adjacent to the post office were encouraged and supported by the city because similar city-sponsored programs worked in another river city, Pittsburgh (and the developer of the Evansville post office had already renovated the old Pittsburgh and Lake Erie railroad station in Pittsburgh). A river walk project was also undertaken, because the project seems to have worked in Cincinnati.

"We don't want to be something we're not," is a refrain heard from nearly all quarters. Roughly translated, these officials mean that the city must encourage economic development in order to raise the standard of living, which is rather low compared to other cities in the nation and even in the region. But no one, they continue, should be under illusions that the city's financing of development projects will fundamentally alter the size or economic base of the city. This is not only, as one top official said, a "reflection of reality that Evansville *can* be no more than what it is," it is also an expression of the vision of the city.

The motto of the city could easily read: Maintain the City in Good Working Order. Indeed, the mayor maintains that he is not interested in the pomp and glitter of opening new buildings and constructing public buildings—a rare quality in a public official. Rather, his emphasis is on renovating the city's aged and decaying infrastructure, a noble stance given the national outcry to address the problems associated with "crumbling infrastructures" but one rooted firmly in Evansville's vision as building a future much like the past. Evansville wants to remain a small, isolated, manufacturing city.

The immediate goal of the city, according to officials, is to improve the quality of life, defined as reducing the levels of unemployment and poverty (historically higher than the national averages), improving cultural and recreational facilities, and establishing a less-volatile, more stable urban economic base. This quality-of-life goal is to be pursued within the overarching constraint of not encouraging population growth or, at a minimum, of not relying on population growth to be the engine for attaining the goal. Evansville's census figures for the year 2010 will probably reveal a population not much different from the 1990 level of 136,000, a level that has changed little in 50 years; and that seems to suit Evansville officials just fine. The aspirations of Evansville's officials indicate relative complacence with the city's position within its relevant system of cities.

Springfield

Although the contemporary fiscal picture of Springfield and the short-term future of its underlying economy appear bleak and dominate policy-makers' discussions about the city's development programs, the city has not been induced to offer incentives to developers or to risk city funds. On the contrary, the prevalent attitude among city officials is that city funds should not be invested or risked in development programs.

The city's operating programs and general administration have been in a slow downward spiral since the mid-1970s. To remove even more city funds from those programs and invest them in development projects in the hopes that employment will improve pushes the bounds of good government behavior, as defined by city residents. Springfield's mayor stated the sentiment clearly: "Springfield residents see incentives as a give-away, and unless 500 or more jobs are created immediately [by a development project], the citizens would be opposed [to any city investment]." The finance director summarized the constraints on the city's vision as a combination of "financial restraints and public perception."

In 1975, when the city went to the voters for a dedicated income tax, city officials presented a clear picture of how the funds were to be invested. Springfield's central business district had been in decline for decades, a decline that accelerated after a large suburban mall opened in 1972. Commercial activity in the downtown was almost nonexistent. Some of the funds from the income tax were to be invested in the city-owned core redevelopment block to make the downtown more attractive to shoppers. To date, however, business establishments have not moved back to the city, and downtown commercial activity and retail sales have not rebounded, so the one long-term plan in which the city has invested has yet to be realized.

City officials' vision of the city is tied closely to its current economic and fiscal position; therefore, it is a short-run vision. Data on employment, income, the school dropout rate, and poverty are discouraging and appear to be getting worse. The vision, then, is one of focusing the city's energies on those factors. This means that there is no long-term plan for economic development to guide the city's investment of resources. Attention is on immediate crises, namely, sharply declining revenues and service levels, shrinking employment opportunities, and declining wage rates. And although "concern" for the declining conditions of the city certainly dominates city officials' vision for the future, the fiscal and political situation of the city precludes the active, aggressive investment of city resources in development projects.

City officials are unwilling to become active in the development process because of fiscal realities and the dominant political culture, which clearly argues for limited government involvement. The city's inactive posture in the investment of city funds for development projects is also due, according to one official, to the "unwillingness of city commissioners to assume any risk" in investing city resources. As far as city officials are concerned, the city is doing as much as it can to stem the tide of declining economic and fiscal conditions by promoting development of the core redevelopment block and by reducing the city's budget and its services to residents. Revitalization, it seems, is up to the private marketplace; public intervention will not become any more dominant nor will the city become any more active in promoting development. If city size and economic importance diminish as a consequence, that's an outcome city officials understand might happen.

CONCLUDING OBSERVATIONS

Local economic development is commonly thought of in terms of job growth and changes in the tax base. And while it certainly contains elements of both, it is at the same time something else. Image, a concept difficult to isolate and quantify, plays a central role in economic development. A city's image is the backdrop against which development occurs; and image creation is frequently a goal of the economic development process. Orlando means Mickey Mouse; Huntsville conveys rockets. And both of those cities have capitalized on these images for economic expansion. In Orlando's case, it is tourism; in Huntsville's, high technology. Sustaining a positive image may be easier than reversing a negative one. Beaumont and Lowell have found image re-creation to be an arduous process, complicated by time lags and persistent misconceptions. Despite the intangibility of image, it remains critical to local economic development.

4 / CITIES AND ECONOMIC DEVELOPMENT

CONVENTIONAL WISDOM insists that, in market economies, unfettered markets allocate resources efficiently. Under certain conditions, government intervention becomes appropriate to correct or improve markets and enhance the efficient properties of markets. These conditions, called market failures, include public goods, externalities, natural monopolies, and informational asymmetries. Nevertheless, *failure* is often defined by officials and policymakers in terms that have little to do with enhancing the efficiency of (macro) markets or in terms that only indirectly respond to the conventional definitions of market failure. Instead, when society perceives that a good is undersupplied or that it is poorly distributed or that "private financial markets fail to incorporate social benefits in decision making",[1] then the market is perceived as having failed and government intervention is perhaps justified. Agricultural subsidies are premised more on ensuring production and buoying farm prices than correcting market failure defined in terms of efficiently working markets. Nor does market failure explain the behavior of cities in providing economic development incentives.

The argument we develop in this chapter is that theoretical market failures do not explain city government efforts to subsidize or spur development, nor do they require or precipitate government response. Rather, purposive government action in promoting economic development is legitimized because the market mechanism has proved itself incapable of providing the right kind of spatial incentive or ensuring the right kind of local competition in the production of certain goods and services that are spatially bound. Macrolevel markets have not failed when cities are in decline; to the contrary, they have succeeded in signaling a better return on investment and more efficient production and consumption at another location. But the political system's control and authority are limited to a finite space, and that space has consequences to the viability of the polity.

A city's influence extends only a small distance from its political boundaries. Perception of market failure by city officials, then, is tied spatially only to the area they control. Public intervention is unsheathed as an important tool to reestablish a city's tax-services equilibrium and to improve its revenue profile. And while government production or its provision of goods and services, especially the promotion of economic development programs, might fail from the perspective of economic efficiency, what constitutes failure is clearly negotiable in the political world.

MARKET FAILURE

Economists contend that because governments distort markets and, as a result, decrease social surplus and impose a deadweight loss upon society, government intervention should occur only when the market is unable to produce and distribute goods efficiently. Another way of stating this is that only after markets have demonstrably failed to behave efficiently should governments actively intercede in the production or distribution process. The contemporary literature identifies four primary types of market failure that tend to be accepted as reasonable premises for government involvement.[2] The first, and the most well known, is public goods. These are goods that are nonexcludable and nonrivalrous, meaning that consumers cannot prevent others from enjoying them and that one person's consumption does not diminish the quantity available to others. Clean air, public safety, and civil rights are examples of these types of goods. Their provision by government agencies is justified because market signals would result in an undersupply of public goods.

A second type of market failure is the existence of natural monopolies. These are producers "whose fixed costs of providing a good are high relative to the variable cost so that average cost declines over the relevant range of demand."[3] Running multiple natural gas pipelines through a city would generally be inefficient and would necessitate government regulation over the provision of natural gas.

A third market failure is externalities, or spillovers. An externality is any impact on a third person or party that results from any action between producers and consumers to which the third party did not consent. Leaking underground storage tanks that pollute drinking water, lowered property values as a result of being located next to unkempt property, and toxic emissions spewed into the atmosphere are examples of this type of market failure. Externalities can also be beneficial.

A fourth market failure is informational asymmetries. Consumers and producers may have different information about a particular product, resulting in inefficient markets if the consumer bids on a product with unknown defects. In other words, if information about a good is not equally available and known to both consumer and producer, government agencies may address the resulting inefficiency through such action as product labeling (or lemon laws, as some states call their regulation of the used car business).

But in addition to market failure related to efficiency, market failure also has come to mean that the price or quantity of a particular good or service is inadequate or inappropriate.[4] Government intervention in these cases is designed to increase the supply (e.g., milk subsidies) or reduce the price (e.g., recreation) of certain goods. In other words, as Richard Musgrave argues in his classic treatise on public finance, government intervention is not solely premised on poorly operating or inefficient markets; rather, when a socially desirable, optimal level of output has not been realized, government intervention—a visible and political response—influences the quantity of the good provided.[5] This response is not a result of the invisible hand of the marketplace; under this line of reasoning, markets fail if society, or more precisely the city's leadership, deems that, say, housing production has fallen below certain societal expectations, or caloric intake does not meet a certain standard, or income and employment levels are below acceptable levels, or downtown retail sales lag behind suburban retail sales, or land values are underpriced, or investment is insufficient, and on and on. As a result, economic efficiency as the justification for government intervention may take a back seat to political expediency and societal or community pressure.

Unless a general economic recession afflicts the entire nation or vast regions of it, city markets in general do not fail in the production and consumption process. Rather, local economic downturns reflect local underlying market forces and production factors—for example, land may be overvalued, labor costs may exceed those of other localities, or the return on investment may be low. More efficient markets exist elsewhere. Migration of firms and people ensue in response to these broader market signals. What is lacking in explaining city intervention in the development process, then, is a framework to categorize market failure. *Space* and *government jurisdiction* have been omitted.

Cities are not mobile. Unlike underutilized or unutilized labor and capital, land cannot (and labor and capital do not necessarily) migrate to high-demand cities and regions. But because cities are competitive with other cities regionally, nationally, and globally, they do invest in their development potential to enhance their prospects.[6]

Santa Barbara, for example, experiences a high demand for land. Therefore, the city begins the development process with a competitive advantage over many other places, namely, the desire of developers to gain access to the market. However, city leaders have grown increasingly sensitive to the negative externalities of development, like demand on water and traffic congestion. In the view of city leaders, a successful Santa Barbara is one that lives within its resources. Thus, the concern for Santa Barbara is that the efficient functioning of the market will ultimately destroy the city's image and character. According to government officials, the city's bright future is predicated on the effective management of growth. Therefore, Santa Barbara offers the unusual case of government closely guarding entry to its market. Santa Barbara asks developers, What will you offer to gain entry to the market? Yet even with very costly artificial barriers to entry, demand remains strong.[7]

City officials who perceive market failure within their jurisdictions have choices: either they invest public capital for the purpose of correcting those perceived failures or they allow the marketplace to allocate resources to their most efficient and profitable location. While the economic interests of cities may parallel those of other production factors, cities have one constraint not shared by people, firms, and investors: they are immobile. Except for the freedom to invest bond proceeds and surplus revenues in accounts not within the city limits (e.g., U.S. Treasury notes, repurchase agreements, and other cash investment options), nearly all other economic decisions are confined to a specific piece of real estate.

City annexation of adjoining territory is one means of softening the immobility condition. The extension of city boundaries is frequently motivated by a desire for additional developable space and the resulting revenues. Cities that can expand, that are not hemmed in by incorporated suburbs, are advantaged. The steady territorial accretion of Boise and Orlando, for example, stand in marked contrast to Lowell's maintenance of long-established boundaries. (Appendix table A.2 displays the territorial sizes of the cities from 1940 to 1990.)

Cities do not intervene in local economies because markets have failed but rather because markets have succeeded. Locations and space may have failed, but migration of labor and capital to more efficient markets—markets that might also have better land prices—should yield a higher quantity of commodities at a lower price. Whether the location for that production is in a nearby region, a neighboring nation, or across the ocean makes no difference to the hidden hand of the spatially neutral market. But it does make a difference to a city with limited territorial authority. A city government might be expected to intervene to enhance both the city's locational advantage and the efficient working of the market.

Consequently, when city leaders perceive market failure, they are faced with a choice of either artificially influencing the market through mobilizing public capital or abiding by the hidden hand. Risks are inherent in either choice. Intervention might fail; it might become an albatross around the city's neck, as was Flint's attempt to spur development through tourism by granting tax credits to an automobile theme park, Auto-World.[8] On the other hand, the uninterrupted exodus from the city in response to market signals, as people and firms vote with their feet, might leave a veritable ghost town in its wake.

GOVERNMENT FAILURE

Once city leaders have decided to invest in the development potential of their city, the project may fail anyway, failure being defined in terms of efficiently allocating resources to meet market demands within the city's jurisdiction. Governments, like markets, are prone to failure—as Charles Wolf argued forcefully more than a decade ago.[9] The crux of his argument—that governments can also fail in their attempts to correct market failure—primarily rests on the fact that market forces usually do not operate, or do not operate effectively, when the government intervenes and therefore do not provide the necessary corrective signals about output, price, and quality.

Government failure, based on the synthetic work of David Weimer and Aidan Vining, can be attributed to at least four factors.[10] First, rent seekers (or lobbyists who attempt to benefit their clients through government intervention or protection) attempt to gain a higher benefit from the government than can be obtained through the market. Returns to rent seekers come at the expense of other groups. Setting prices administratively, for example, results theoretically in lower output and a deadweight loss to society compared with market-determined prices. Furthermore, returns from investments protected from competition by government regulation are higher than returns from investments in the open market. In the case of urban development projects, developers sometimes are armed with "confidential" information about a needed subsidy and encourage city development investment levels above what would have been acceptable in the marketplace.[11]

Second, governments impute value to output on the basis of input costs rather than let the market give value to the outcome, since no market valuation is possible. Because most public agencies do not subject their products to the discipline of the marketplace, the value of the product is imputed. The value of output is defined not by consumer demand but by input costs. Whatever the good or service costs to produce is assumed to be its value to the community, which does not necessarily provide signals to the government that could result in more efficient production or a lower price. The market's absence in providing discipline to the producer (the city government) consequently might result in inefficient production.[12]

Third, governments are monopolies and not necessarily efficient. The profit motive and competition encourages private, market-oriented firms to innovate and to become efficient. Monopolies, such as a government, experience little or no competition for many of their products. This does not mean that public agencies cannot innovate; indeed, bureaucrats' career incentives frequently encourage innovation. Rather, the motivating factor behind innovation and product improvement is neither profit nor market competition; thus efficiency gains are problematic at best. As a consequence, "the absence of competition raises the possibility that public agencies can survive even if they fail to operate efficiently."[13]

The last form of government failure falls under the rubric of fiscal externalities, which are tax benefits captured by other governments but not paid for by them. Besides the well-worn examples of public safety services provided to commuters and visitors, development projects are illustrative of this form of government failure. Development projects tend to benefit a broader spatial arena and other neighboring government jurisdictions than just the jurisdiction that facilitated and paid for those projects. Employment and income benefits of development projects leak out of the investor's political jurisdiction and seep into other political jurisdictions. Housing values and the subsequent capture of tax revenues by suburban school districts and bedroom communities are lost benefits to the jurisdiction that made the investment and risked its resources. To capture those fiscal externalities, participation by higher levels of government clearly becomes appropriate, as do other forms of compensation by the beneficiary communities. But even with tremendous fiscal spillover and little or no higher-level government subsidy to capture those externalities, cities continue to invest resources in development.

The government's analog to the private market's failure-of-information asymmetry is what the public choice literature calls fiscal illusion, which contends that the actual costs of producing goods can be hidden from taxpayers through a variety of mechanisms.[14] Bureaucrats, as rational, self-interested individuals, do not reveal the true costs of programs and exaggerate their benefits. Because they, like their private sector counterparts in negotiations with government agencies, possess information that is either unavailable or difficult to retrieve by legislators and the general public, funding levels for those government agencies tend to be unrelated to any objective measure of performance. Moreover, it is to the advantage of agencies and bureaucrats to maintain confusion in the minds of voters and legislators about service delivery responsibility and tax burden. Blame for service failure can be deflected to other agencies and bureaucrats. Voters and city leaders, without this information, make uninformed and thus inefficient choices of tax policy and services as a result.

The public's perception of government failures in a host of service delivery areas has resulted in reconceptualizing the government's role—or reinventing government. Ted Kolderie argues that, by separating the production of a good or service from its provision, a number of public-private cooperative options exist for cities to consider. Provision refers to the "policy decision that a benefit or service will be made available, to whom and at what level." Production, on the other hand, refers to the "actual arrangement for its organization and delivery."[15] Cities, therefore, can opt out of their production responsibilities while maintaining control (the provision function) over the producer's delivery of the service. According to Vining and Weimer, "if, given public financing, supply is not contestable [defined as effective competition for supply of the good], then the government should produce the good itself. If, given public financing, supply is perfectly contestable, then government should procure the good through contracting." Government provision of a service "is appropriate when market failures or other explicit goals justify government supply and supply of the good is not contestable. In cases where supply is partially contestable, the magnitude of the risk of opportunism should determine whether production is by government, nonprofit organizations, or private firms."[16]

This perspective, however, leaves little room for the kind of intervention cities decide on in their development function. Certainly there is no (global) market failure when cities invest in their development function and the supply of the good (development incentives) is clearly contestable—albeit in another spatial market area. In other words, the advice for government production hinges on efficiency and competition when territoriality does not matter. But to cities, territoriality does matter. The question of contestability requires analysis from two planes. From a macro or national level, city development programs are inefficient. The local marketplace may have "failed," but the larger marketplace is sending signals to the local marketplace that the latter has higher comparative costs than producing a good elsewhere. City government production of development incentives only moves investment capital or supply from more productive locations within the larger society to the city. Not only does this activity transfer wealth, especially if it involves federal or state grants for the project, it further subsidizes inefficiency. On this plane, then, supply is contestable, so city governments should stay out.

But if we analyze contestability on a second plane, we get different policy implications. In small-region, or micro, markets with declining returns on capital investment, the supply of the good (investment capital) might not be contestable, or not to the satisfaction of city officials, whose view of the market extends only to the city's boundaries. If contestability is not in question, government production is certainly warranted. Markets are not spaceless, and government decisions are usually confined to a small territory. City government production of incentives in the form of investment capital or opportunities, therefore, is admissible at this level of analysis because of the issue of their contestability in micromarkets.

GOVERNMENT MARKET FAILURE:
FAILURE OF A THIRD KIND

Since the late 1970s, both market and government failure have become widely accepted as rationales for first government intervention and then government withdrawal or government partnerships with the private sector. One of the great theorems of city governance in the 1980s and 1990s is the following: If market failure makes government intervention necessary, government failure has made a return to the market imperative. Combinations of public and private operations, contracting out, private production and public provision, and other eclectic organizational responses to perceived market and government failures of the past have been tried as means of improving both efficiency and the probability of successful economic development.[17]

Cities, consequently, have found themselves in an interesting quandary: cities intervene because of perceived market failure in efficiently allocating goods and services to meet individual preferences, and yet cities can themselves fail because of a lack of pure market signals about the allocation of goods and services in order to satisfy collective preferences. The argument that governments fail because they do not read market signals properly is ironic because it negates the entire premise for their intervention to begin with, namely, that the market was faulty in the first place.

As a consequence of a host of factors, tax revolts became the sine qua non of state and local politics since California's Proposition 13 in 1978 and Massachusetts' Proposition 2½ in 1980. In response, marketlike pricing mechanisms were introduced or augmented for a host of government services, ranging from jails to garbage. The pay-for-it-yourself sentiment of the voter-taxpayer meant that they could match their consumption of government services with charges and adjust their consumption to meet their individual preferences. Divining the collective preference, which is assigned to local legislative bodies, became an increasingly less important role of government agencies, as the invisible hand of the marketplace gradually assumed cities' allocational responsibilities. The voter-taxpayer sends signals to the government as provider of goods and services in a manner analogous to consumers sending signals to producers through the marketplace.

Conventional wisdom today has shifted significantly from the earlier era. General taxes supply increasingly less revenue to city governments for services as a result of the public's perception of government failure (namely, that the government does not rely enough on markets to properly evaluate government production of goods and services). Increasingly, as technology and data have proliferated, governments have been better able to measure the quantity of a specific government service consumed by an individual or family or firm. Measures of consumption can easily be compared with the tax price of that government service, and voter-taxpayers can effectively monitor whether they receive an appropriate array of services for that tax price.

Fees, charges, coproduction with the private sector, contracting out, all have a similar characteristic, namely, they avoid or at least minimize the probability of government failure by introducing at least a modicum of market discipline. A market price on government services should force consumers to reveal their true preferences, leading in turn to an efficient allocation of resources or, at least, to minimizing long-term oversupply of the service as a consequence of artificially low prices. A fee-based pricing structure should encourage more rational consumption behavior compared to a general tax-based financing structure. Consumer-taxpayers should demand only the quantity of those public services they can afford (that is, their ability to pay constrains their consumption), and general tax revenues would not necessarily be required to subsidize their needs.

Whether these pricing mechanisms in fact improve efficiency may be debatable; that they are pursued vigorously is not (see table 4.1). As a fiscal policy option in the aftermath of Proposition 13 and other tax limitation measures around the nation, marketlike mechanisms remain strong. A survey of 408 cities found that, between 1980 and 1983, the most frequently employed revenue-enhancing strategy was to increase user fees, a strategy employed by 83 percent of the responding cities.[18] Likewise, according to the annual fiscal condition surveys of the National League of Cities, 67 percent of all responding cities in 1988 increased fees and charges, and 37 percent introduced new fees and charges. By 1991, as mounting economic pressure pushed city after city toward the brink of fiscal crisis, 73 percent increased fees and charges and 40 percent implemented new fees and charges.[19]

In addition to expanding marketlike pricing strategies, cities also expand their development programs into areas once considered too risky for the public sector. Susan Clarke and Gary Gaile argue that, since 1980, cities' development programs have been "characterized by a stronger investment and entrepreneurial approach; the use of revolving loan funds, below market loans, and program income indicates generation of reve-

Table 4.1

Sources of City Revenue, 1977–1991 (percentage of total revenue)

Source	1977	1979	1981	1983	1985	1987	1989	1991
User fees	14.5	16.1	18.3	20.0	21.1	21.9	21.3	21.8
Utility revenue	14.5	15.8	17.2	17.8	17.8	17.0	17.2	16.3
Taxes	35.3	33.1	32.3	32.1	32.3	32.6	34.6	34.3

Source: Bureau of the Census, *City Government Finances* (Washington, D.C.: Government Printing Office, various years).

nue streams independent of federal programs and tax revenues. . . . And attention to markets and business start-ups—two hallmarks of entrepreneurial approaches—also characterizes this new postfederal era."[20] These entrepreneurial approaches to economic development, rooted as they are in a disciplined market structure, are quite different from earlier approaches.

That local government provision of goods and services in a marketlike manner will result in a third kind of failure is highly probable. Market failure for governments, as opposed to market failure for private goods—such as demand for greater supply of a government service for the same price or demand for the same quantity of the service at a lower price—might be the primary form of failure in the future. When market failure is detected, the city may be motivated to respond in one of two ways. Either the city immediately intervenes to support the firm or individual and tries to ensure that the market will no longer fail (e.g., through subsidy, tax abatement, loans, or infrastructure provision); or the city supplies the needed facility and risks its own funds in the hope of generating a profit without entangling other individuals or firms. The former describes a city as subsidizer and expediter, the latter a city as investor. Either choice enmeshes the city with the private sector to a greater or lesser degree. Consequently, the possibility of both market failure and government failure exists.

Two case studies follow. The first illustrates the entanglement of market-cum-government failure when the city assumes the role of a subsidizer. The second illustrates market and government failure when the city behaves as an investor.

City as Subsidizer: Springfield's City Market and Hotel

Springfield's 1980 master plan identified the City Market area as needing immediate attention. The project was conceived in 1982 as a market and office space to be housed in one building, the old City Market. The first floor of the old building had housed a city market for nearly a century; the second and third floors were city government offices. The city owned the building and the land. Across the street is the Arcade Building, which was to be restored and was to house 24 factory outlet/off-price retailers.

Two developers came forward with proposals and asked the city to apply for a $1,645,000 urban development action grant (UDAG). But soon after the UDAG application was approved, the deal unraveled. The City Market portion of the project continued, but the developer of the Arcade experienced severe financial hardship and backed out. The $600,000 UDAG loan for the Arcade was then held in abeyance by the Department of Housing and Urban Development for six years until another project on the same site attracted a developer. At the time, the city did not actively consider financing the project from its own funds other than dedicated funds associated with the city's core redevelopment program designed to stimulate the central business district. These funds consisted of a tax-increment financing district (for parking), property tax abatement (which loads the costs onto the school district and county because the city almost completely depends upon the income tax), and federal funds from a community development block grant (CDBG) and UDAG. These were the public investment portions of the City Market project.

The cost of the three-phase project, excluding the library and small transit center, was $11.5 million. The first phase was the rehabilitation of the City Market building. Private investors put up nearly $2.5 million, and the city loaned the developers $311,000 from its CDBG and $550,000 from UDAG funds. A second phase was designed to realign the Conrail railroad tracks adjacent to the project site and to expand public parking for the City Market.[21] More than $600,000 in private funds from the railroad company were raised for this phase of the project, $1 million was contributed from CDBG, and UDAG funds covered the remaining $495,000. Those two phases, the City Market and the parking lot and railroad alignment projects, were completed by 1988.

The Community Investment Corporation (CIC), a nonprofit corporation affiliated with the city, was granted CDBG funds to loan to the City Market developer. The amount of the loan was $311,000, to be repaid to CIC over 15 years at 9 percent interest and an annual service fee of 1 percent of the outstanding principal. UDAG loans from the city amounted to $550,000 at 7 percent interest. The developer asked to start loan payments to CIC at the end of 1985 ($39,943 per year); by 1989, the developer was behind in payments by at least $10,000. The UDAG loan repayment has been deferred since 1987.

Because the land and building are leased to the developer from the city, no property taxes are due from the developer, but the developer does pay into a tax-equivalency fund an amount equal to the property tax bill if the project were not located on tax-exempt property. That in-lieu-of payment amounts to approximately $28,000 annually. Even though contributions to the tax-equivalency fund are paid in lieu of property taxes and the city's portion is practically nonexistent, the city's tax-equivalency fund receives the entire amount for core redevelopment programs.[22]

The final phase of the project was to have been reconstruction of the Arcade, but because of a sharp downturn in the state's economy in 1982 and 1983, the developer who initially agreed to take on the Arcade project experienced financial difficulties and backed out. No other developer could be induced to replace him until 1988. Between 1982 and 1988, the Arcade was in dire need of major repairs, especially to the roof. Consequently, the city, which purchased the building as part of its core redevelopment program, invested nearly $0.6 million in repairs until a new developer could be found. By 1988, however, the city decided that in the "interests of public health and safety" the structure had to be razed. After a lengthy struggle—preservationists wanted the structure to be renovated—the building came down in 1988 to make room for a new hotel.

The city sold the cleared site to a developer for a dollar, a clear indication that the opportunity costs associated with keeping the property for a future developer were extraordinary. The tax-equivalency fund contributed $313,350 for razing the building, relocating the tenants, and providing parking spaces. The city's public improvement fund contributed $284,495 to the project. The public improvement fund investment and other city investment of $284,000 for repairing and razing the structure represent the city's investment, excluding federal contributions (see table 4.2). The new developer of the hotel complex invested approximately $3.5 million.[23] In addition, the developer borrowed $600,000 from the original 1983 UDAG award. The city invested CDBG funds of $1 million over a 10-year period for acquisition, roof repair, heating, and cooling repairs, and tenant relocation.

By all indicators, the City Market has not drawn many people downtown. In fact, the developers of the City Market asked to postpone their

Table 4.2
Investment in Springfield's City Market and Hotel
(thousands of current dollars)

Phase	Public Investment	Private Investment
Rehabilitation	861	2,483
UDAG loan	550	
CDBG	311	
Amenities	1,474	657
UDAG grant (RR alignment)	450	
CDBG (RR alignment)	333	
CDBG (parking)	691	
Hotel	2,493	3,500
CDBG	1,011	
TIF (tax equivalency fund)	313	
PI	285	
Other	284	
UDAG	600	
Total	4,828	6,640

Source: Files, City Manager's Office, Springfield. Data are as of April 11, 1989. The private portion of the hotel costs are estimates.

Note: The marketplace was granted an in-lieu-of-payment to the city in exchange for abating property taxes; therefore, there are no costs to the city. In fact, the city receives more revenues because the entire abated property tax is owed to the city, rather than to all local governments. Costs associated with construction of the public library are excluded from this summary, even though the city considers the library an integral part of the City Market project. The initial CDBG loan was made in 1979 for $354,750 for acquiring the arcade. In 1981–82, another $553,249 was invested in repair and heating and cooling. During 1981–85, $102,980 was used for relocation.

loan payments to the city until 1992 because of poor sales. Furthermore, there are no signs of renovated buildings in the adjacent area. Building permits for a one-block radius around the City Market are almost non-existent, according to city officials. Both indicators suggest that any indirect benefits from the project have not been realized.

One immediate benefit of the project is the surrogate property tax payments, otherwise known as the in-lieu-of payment. The City Market is on tax-exempt property owned by the city. In exchange for renting the property, developers agreed to contribute a property tax equivalent into the tax-equivalency fund of approximately $27,000 annually. This contribution can be used for other projects in the core redevelopment area and amounts to a profit for the city, given that if the same project were located on taxable property, the city would receive virtually no property tax. If the city indeed reaps the predicted $71,250 in income taxes from the hotel project and the $27,000 in in-lieu-of payments, the $285,000 city investment (from the public improvement fund) would be repaid within three years of the hotel's ribbon-cutting ceremonies. Indeed, the expectation was that the city would reap a substantial return on its initial investment by the end of 1994 (the hotel opened in 1991). Comparing the city's direct and indirect costs (i.e., tax-equivalency fund contributions of $313,000) associated with the purchase, renovating, and razing the Old Arcade, the city's return on investment will not become positive until the year 2000, at the earliest.

City as Investor: Lowell's Kerouac Park

The Lowell Heritage State Park was provided $3.1 million in state funds to develop an open space next to a canal near the confluence of the Merrimack and Concord Rivers and adjacent to several textile mills. The state also contributed $700,000 for a commemoration to Lowell's native son, beat author Jack Kerouac. The state contracted with the city to implement the project. The purposes of the $3.8-million state grant were twofold: (1) to acquire and raze the Curran-Morton warehouse, which the city felt could not be preserved and reused because of its six-foot ceilings and (2) to build a memorial to Kerouac. The city's purpose was much grander. By razing the warehouse, old textile mills behind the warehouse would have the space needed for conversion into condominiums. The project, according to city memoranda, should have cost only $3.5 million. The balance of nearly $300,000, according to the agreement with the state, was to have been applied to other canal projects within the city. Lowell ran into a lawsuit instead.

The city supported the demolition of the Curran-Morton warehouse. In a memorandum from the city manager to the city council dated January 16, 1985, the city manager contended that "from the City's perspective, this state-funded project will not only assume a continuation of our revitalization effort by providing 3,000–4,000 new job opportunities for our residents [by rehabilitating the mills into condominiums] but will also add a significant piece of new public open space to the Lowell Heritage State Park and Lowell National Historical Park System." The city then took the property through an eminent domain action on March 17, 1986, paying the owner its appraised value of $900,000. The owner did not want to sell because he thought he could develop the warehouse into boutique stores. Nevertheless, a demolition contract was let, and between November 12, 1986, and January 26, 1987, the building was razed.

The new open space was precisely what other developers, as well as the city, were looking for. The planning and development director at the time claims that, before the warehouse was razed, he took 35 developers through the sprawling Massachusetts Mill complex on the opposite side of the Concord River from the warehouse and could not interest one of them in renovating the mill. Once the warehouse was razed, a developer stepped in immediately. Indeed, two mills near the open space were re-developed as a direct consequence of the warehouse's demolition (Massachusetts Mill and Boott Mill). A letter from the attorney for both mills to the city manager clearly stated the importance of the open space: "But for the fact that public authorities are presently condemning and raising [sic] this Store House and creating a parklike open space on the site, all at no cost to us, Niuna-Lowell, Inc. [the developers] would have terminated its development plans."

Nevertheless, the original owner was not satisfied with the city's action and sued the city, claiming that the now-demolished warehouse had been worth $3 million. To illustrate his point, he took the jury one block from the site of his former warehouse to the Hilton Hotel and proclaimed that he had intended all along to develop the property along the same lines as Hilton. A jury, in August 1988, agreed with the owner, meaning that with interest and the 1986 payment of $900,000 the city still owed nearly $2.5 million. The state's agreement with the city, meanwhile, was clear that any additional costs were the city's responsibility. So the city, unable to raise property taxes to cover the cost, dipped into its end-of-year cash balances.

According to two former city planning and development directors, not only was the $2.5-million court-imposed investment worth it, but the city would have invested in it even if the final cost could have been known in advance. The investment is seen by these officials much like a UDAG (in line with the attorney's argument, with which city officials seem to acquiesce). Namely, without the city's investment of $2.5 million (albeit an unplanned investment), the $60-million private investment in Massachusetts Mills would not have happened; but for the eminent domain-taking by the city, Massachusetts Mills would never have happened.

The development of Kerouac Park has opened a vista in the city's central business district unlike that of any other city project. Open space of any kind is rare in this densely built city. The uninterrupted mile of textile mills no more than five stories high characterizes this old mill town. Before the demolition of the Curran-Morton warehouse, a state official declared the area around Massachusetts Mills the most visually depressing he had ever seen. To a visitor accustomed to lower-density commercial and residential areas, even the new open space might appear insufficient. But to the developers who renovated the mills into condominiums, the little bit of open space was enough to warrant their risking an investment of nearly $60 million. The view from the condominiums across the canal includes the Kerouac Commemorative Park.

DEVELOPMENT TOOLS

Whether as expediters or subsidizers or any other kind of investor, city officials can choose from a veritable cornucopia of incentives, inducements, and giveaways. Some of these development tools are considered fairly routine; that is, there is little public debate about the appropriateness of the incentive because it is considered standard fare for the city. Other tools are more complex, requiring extensive consideration and public assessment of their appropriateness. (We speak now not of the consideration about where the project is to be located, which would entail an assessment of the neighborhood's willingness to accept a project, but about the appropriateness of financial incentives.) A general discussion of city development incentives follows; an analysis of each city's development tools appears in appendix B.

The Financial Component

Cities tend to regard some incentives as routine. Other incentives are not. Developers contact city planning and development offices and ask what financial incentives the city has to offer, and city officials then select from a host of development tools, combining them into bundles. This standard fare can be grouped into four bundles: direct investment, indirect subsidies, assistance, and no risk. Inherent in each bundle is greater or lesser risk to the city's treasury. City development tools assume a variety of shapes and sizes, some requiring complex bond-issuing regulations, others that are simple cash transfers and minor infrastructure provision, and still others that become legal entanglements. Inherent in each tool is a monetary or financial commitment of city revenue. At one extreme is the direct investment of city funds and the inherent fiscal risk to the city; at the other extreme are projects that require no city investment and rely, instead, on state or federal funding.

In direct investment, a city contributes cash to a development project— from the general fund in the form of infrastructure provision and through issuing general obligation bonds. It thus makes a firm investment in the project and assumes a fairly substantial financial risk. Because of the scarce and competitive nature of this resource, this kind of investment signifies that other potential projects cannot be financed.

Indirect subsidies refer to present-value subsidies and value-creating subsidies.[24] These include making below-market loans to developers, granting density bonuses, purchasing land, razing structures, granting tax abatement, and giving tax incentives, all clearly involving financial risk for the city. Present-value subsidies, such as below-market loans and tax abatement, represent unrealized and future costs to the city. Although it is not a direct allocation from the city's budget, this does not represent a zero-sum tax game—once it has been offered does not mean city revenues are unavailable for other projects. The subsidy represents forgone revenues and financial risk. Value-creating subsidies, such as sale of city-owned land and offerings of density bonuses to residential developers, are financial risks much like tax abatement. The city does not earn income from these tools unless they are employed in the development process. They create value after their mobilization for development. Financial risk, therefore, is not immediate and does not require an appropriation from the city's budget. Project success or failure does not damage the financial integrity of the city's budget. Value-creating subsidies represent a financial risk much like tax abatement.

The category called assistance allows government-assisted entrance to market-type funds. These development costs are absorbed by users and beneficiaries (developers) directly, even though they do not represent direct private outlays of the firm or of individuals and include such commonplace tools as city-issued industrial revenue bonds, tax-increment financing bonds, or fee-based financing of sewer and water infrastructure. These forms of government finance allow private developers access to city utilities or to the tax-exempt bond market and represent little financial risk to the city.

The no-risk category requires no city investment and relies instead on state or federal funding; cities do not have to exchange resources for those projects and in turn do not have to trade off one city project for another. These projects, consequently, pose little financial risk to a city's budget.

We created a seven-point index of the bundles in these four groups as follows:

0= No risk
1= Assistance; or assistance and no risk
2= Subsidies; or subsidies and no risk
3= Subsidies and assistance; or subsidies, assistance, and no risk
4= Investment; or investment and no risk
5= Investment and assistance; or investment, assistance, and no risk
6= Investment and subsidies; or investment, subsidies, and no risk
7= Investment, subsidies, and assistance; or investment, subsidies, assistance, and no risk

For illustrative purposes, table 4.3 provides comparative data from the study cities, using the seven-point index of development incentives and two types of development incentive packages, routine and complex.[25] (The details of the development tools used by the study cities can be found in appendix B.) The bundle of incentives offered suggests that even if a city's fiscal condition or aspirations encouraged its participation in the development process, its attempts at addressing the causes of these underlying triggers did not result in substantial risk of public resources. Yet it is also clear that a city's offering of routine incentives risked less of its own resources than when they involved complex projects. The potential risk associated with complex development projects involving federal or state funds might appear, then, to be scattered across more entities and therefore discounted by city officials. Should a development project

Table 4.3

Level of Financial Risk, Development Incentive Packages of the Study Cities

Development Incentive Package[a]	Number of Incentive Packages at Each Level of Financial Risk							
	0	1	2	3	4	5	6	7
Routine	0	2	6	0	14	2	2	0
Complex	0	2	1	2	4	1	1	3

Note: Percentage of routine packages at lowest risk (0–2) is 31; at medium risk (3–4), 54; and at highest risk (5–7), 15. Percentage of complex packages at lowest risk is 21; at medium risk, 43; and at highest risk, 36.

a. See note 26 for a definition of *routine* and *complex*.

fail, blame would be spread. Routine projects, on the other hand, seem to be associated with lower levels of risk to the city's finances.

Cities experiencing some degree of economic stress seem to rely on a less risky mix of incentives than more healthy cities (see table 4.4). No routine projects could be classified in the most risky category (i.e., index ratings of 5–7) in economically stressed cities, while one in three routine projects in the healthy cities fell in this risky category. Further, almost one-fourth of the routine projects in cities that aspire to a higher level in their city's system of cities were in the most risky category, compared to a tenth of the projects in cities that don't entertain such aspirations. The data suggest that economically stressed cities and cities without visions of moving up in their system of cities select projects that reduce financial risk to the city and, consequently, reduce the possibility of government failure. Healthy cities and aspiring cities, on the other hand, appear to be not as concerned. The prospects of government failure or failures of the third kind are not daunting. As we show in chapter 5, this tentative conclusion might inhere in the fact that healthy cities can take the risk because the prospects of success are quite good and that aspiring cities must take the risk because these projects are instrumental in the move from one level in their hierarchy to another.

The Organizational Component

The perception of market failure and the threat of government failure have led cities to engage in organizational innovation. Seeking a structure that can bridge the gap between the public and private sectors, cities have created an array of formal partnerships. These include downtown development boards, development corporations, redevelopment agencies, and any number of other structures that link government and business. These organizational adjustments are justified in terms of "facilitating the economic development process," "operating more efficiently," and "encouraging entrepreneurial behavior." To a large extent, they offer means by which public and private dollars can be effectively commingled. In some instances, they buffer the development process from city politics. The range of their authority varies. The most powerful organizations have eminent domain authority and debt-issuance capability. The most successful—those flush with investment capital and a savvy staff—frequently eclipse the city government that created them. These quasi-public institutions have become the central deal makers in the development process.

Table 4.4

Level of Financial Risk, Routine Incentive Packages of the Study Cities

Type of City	Number of Development Projects at Level of Financial Risk		
	0–2	3–4	5–7
Economically distressed	7	7	0
Economically healthy	1	7	4
Cities with higher-order aspirations	1	5	2
Cities without such aspirations	7	9	2

Note: The UDAG distress index was used to rate cities. See Department of Housing and Urban Development, "Large City and Urban County Universe List," computer printout, 1987.

Others, however, function as specialized subsets of city government, differing from a regular line agency in only the degree of private-sector involvement.

Lowell, with its hybridized intersectoral arrangements, is illustrative of a city where public-private organizations dominate the development scene. In 1979, the Lowell Plan, Inc., was created by Senator Paul Tsongas, Congressman James Shannon, and City Manager B. Joseph Tully to "foster and develop the concept that through the cooperative effort of the municipal government and by the investment from private individuals and private firms of private funds and zeal into private development projects within the City of Lowell, Massachusetts, the City of Lowell shall continue its return to preeminence as the foremost middle-sized city in the United States." Since then, the Lowell Plan has been incorporated as a nonprofit organization. Given its charter, the Lowell Plan has become the focal point of nearly every major development effort within the city.

The Lowell Plan, Inc., convenes regular meetings of key players from the private and public sectors. The purpose is to keep channels of communication open between potential investors and the city government. The meetings are not subject to public scrutiny, and discussions on the city's economic prospects, according to participants, are much more candid and honest than most public meetings. Membership on the Lowell Plan's board of directors is limited to 22 individuals, representing over 150 individual and organizational members, among whom are bankers, developers, attorneys, a newspaper publisher, and educators, along with three public officials (the mayor, the planning and development director, and the city manager). The Lowell Plan acts less as a mediator between the public and private sectors than as an expediter and promoter of development. Its offices are offered to both parties any time a need arises to discuss development and the future economic well-being of the city.

The Lowell Development and Financial Corporation (LDFC) was established in 1975 by a special act of the Massachusetts legislature. LDFC, a nonprofit 501(c)(3) corporation, is owned by 25 stockholders (individuals, community organizations, and financial institutions) and was created to stimulate private investment and economic development. LDFC focuses its efforts on the revitalization of Lowell's downtown by providing "low-interest loans for rehabilitation of historic properties in conformance to the [National] Park theme."[26] LDFC provides secondary mortgage financing at below-market interest rates for industrial, commercial, and residential development.

LDFC also has been given the responsibility of managing the city's UDAG loan repayment program. Developers who borrow from the UDAG repayment fund at below-market interest rates repay the debt to LDFC, not to the city. LDFC is empowered by the city to reinvest those funds in industrial, commercial, and residential projects. In many cases, LDFC is empowered to draw down the loan repayment fund for projects it deems important without city council approval.[27] Developers and other individuals seeking LDFC funds for industrial or commercial purposes must propose renovation or construction projects; total project costs must exceed $300,000, and the loan cannot exceed 25 percent of project cost, or $250,000, whichever is less. The interest rate on the loan is set at 40 percent of the prime lending rate. Loans from LDFC for residential or neighborhood purposes cannot exceed 40 percent of project costs, and the interest rate is also set at 40 percent of the prime.

A former city planning and development director explained that LDFC was the first citywide forum that brought bankers together in a common room to discuss their perceptions of investment projects, risk, and the future of the city. LDFC acts as an informal club in which aspirations, deals, fears, and moral support can be openly, yet privately, expressed among the city's pivotal investor group.

Although LDFC is not a legal partner of the Lowell Plan, the linkage between the two nonprofit organizations is more than casual. The executive director of the Lowell Plan is also the executive director of the LDFC. Consequently, the financial organization (LDFC) knows exactly what the city and developers are contemplating in terms of the city's future (the Lowell Plan). This marriage between two powerful nonprofit organizations—one an investor, the other an organized facilitator of public-private development efforts—results in a situation whereby most of the significant development issues are acted upon in a relatively expeditious manner. Indeed, a key raison d'être for establishing the Lowell Plan is to streamline the development process—to eliminate red tape, as city officials explained—so that private developers and investors do not miss the crucial window of opportunity.

In the Lowell case, the level of intersectoral interaction is high. In Boise and Evansville, the absence of like organizations might suggest that the public and private sectors do not interact. That conclusion is erroneous, however. Both Boise and Evansville have informal partnerships, or regimes, that guide the development process. Furthermore, Boise has reconstituted its redevelopment authority beyond the traditional public proprietary model; Evansville's, on the other hand, has not.[28] What some cities have done is simply formalize existing informal relationships by creating development authorities and corporations. Dennis Judd and Michael Parkinson remind us that "the emergence of an elite constellation or coalition that can speak for a city," one that can take purposive actions, is a key to community survival.[29] Both Huntsville's and Orlando's development authorities formalize a cluster of elites into authoritative, debt-issuing organizations. And Independence entered into a joint venture with the local Chamber of Commerce to create the Independence Committee for Economic Development.

Santa Barbara, however, has purposely avoided the creation of quasi-public organizational structures. Instead, city government remains the locus of economic development decisionmaking, with extensive input from the public.[30] Santa Barbara uses a citizen-focused, decentralized structure, in which the economic development function is housed in the Community Development Office. Santa Barbara encourages citizen participation in government and has a citizen-led planning tradition. Revising the city's comprehensive plan was a sequential undertaking, which built consensus around the theme of resource balance. This community-inspired theme dominates the development (or nondevelopment) process. Leadership comes from coalitions of relatively like-minded individuals, who desire to maintain Santa Barbara's quality of life and its prosperity.

CONCLUDING OBSERVATIONS

Market failure is not a satisfactory explanation for city development behavior. A more compelling rationale lies in the failure of location and space. City governments intervene and risk government failure, taking on roles as subsidizer or investor. Government action is legitimized because the market mechanism has not provided the politically acceptable spatial incentives or ensured the right kind of local competition. City officials hope to regain lost spatial market shares and therefore reduce fiscal stress or expand market shares and move to a new position in the relevant system of cities.

In pursuing development, cities have an array of financial instruments and organizational arrangements at their disposal. How they mobilize them on behalf of a development objective may affect the success of the endeavor. The next two chapters address just that point.

5 / MEASURING SUCCESSFUL DEVELOPMENT

CITY INVESTMENT IN development projects is a purposive decision. Development projects are selected and financial tools are mobilized to pursue some vision of the city. The actual attainment of those visions of the city beautiful is not automatic. White elephants are just as possible as success stories, yet what constitutes a white elephant or a successful development project is not always clear. The purposes of this chapter are to identify different approaches to measuring project success, to identify commonalities among diverse development tools (relying on illustrative data from 40 development projects), and to offer interpretations based on the illustrative data.

City officials agree to intervene in the marketplace for reasons other than enhancing the efficiency of an abstract, spaceless market. Territory matters, and as a consequence, what city leaders look for in a project may appear to be rather perverse in an economic sense. Success is seldom defined in terms of economic efficiency. Intervention to correct a perceived market failure is undertaken by cities either to generate revenue (as an investor) or to address some particular aspect of market failure as defined in the context of the city's jurisdictional limits (as a subsidizer or expediter). Whether the investment is efficient or optimal according to one's definition of investment objectives often becomes nearly irrelevant to city leaders' decision to subsidize a particular project.[1] To assess a project's success given such a viewpoint becomes meaningless. Rather, a project's success in addressing a perceived market failure identified by

officials at the time the project was undertaken should become the benchmark by which success or failure is measured.

Likewise, optimal return on investment for those city projects designed
to generate revenues often becomes a less useful standard against which
to measure success than city officials' own revenue-generating benchmark.
In other words, definitions of success and failure depend on city officials'
motives and on the spatial context of the project. In this chapter, we
analyze the success or failure of the following 40 development projects:

- Beaumont
    Stedman Warehouse renovation   Julie Rogers Theater
    Riverfront Park   Texas Energy Museum

- Boise
    Greenbelt   Towne Square mall
    Downtown core   Boise research center

- Duluth
    Lake Superior Paper Industries   Storefront renovation
    Fitger's Brewery   Fond-du-Luth casino

- Evansville
    Walnut Centre   Bristol-Myers
    T. J. Maxx   Roberts stadium

- Huntsville
    Research Park West   Hampton Cove
    Chrysler/Acu-star   Road improvements

- Independence
    Independence Square   Historic properties
    Truman Road industrial park   Noland Fashion Square mall

- Lowell
    Hilton Hotel   Kerouac Park
    Wannalancit Mills   Stedman Street Industrial Park

- Orlando
    Church Street Station   Callahan Oaks apartments
    Omni Hotel   Wellington apartments

- Santa Barbara
    Paseo Nuevo retail project   La Colina housing project
    Lower State Street improve-   Red Lion Hotel and Confer-
        ments   ence Center

- Springfield
    City Market and hotel   Skalny Basket
    Civic Center   Cooper Industries

MARKET FAILURE AND
GOVERNMENT SUCCESS

As illustrations from previous chapters demonstrate, the definition of project success varies across cities. Success depends on whether the project was intended to show that, for example, Duluth Is Back! or whether, as in the Kerouac Park case, the project was supposed to generate a profit. Success can be measured, for example, as a city's financial return on investment. Projects that generate a profit or revenue for the city's treasury might be deemed successful or considered efficient uses of public resources; others might be considered failures. Whether to attribute employment and income gains to a development project is, at best, controversial. Often, development projects attract firms from one part of the city to another, resulting in no net employment gain. Furthermore, ascertaining what portion of the employment and income gains can be attributed to the development project is difficult at best.

We proceed on the following basis: although a city may or may not be able to increase employment and income, it can influence the value of urban land through zoning regulations, investment decisions, and other means. These policies are pursued to enhance land value, attract private investment, and ultimately to bring greater tax revenue to the city. Higher revenues allow the city to either maintain or improve its tax-services equilibrium. Consequently, although we did not attempt to measure employment and income gains from these development projects, we did measure gains in private investment in the city.

Success is measured according to whether the project accomplished what city leaders wanted the project to accomplish, even if the project was not monetarily profitable. Knowledge of decisionmakers' perceptions about how projects might move the city toward their vision is crucial to an understanding of the basis on which projects should be judged successes or failures: "Although it would appear that much of the selection of policy [tools] is done through familiarity, political tradition, or professional bias, it is still extremely important to know what decisionmakers believe they are getting when they choose one instrument rather than another."[2] The measurement of government success and failure, then, should be against the a priori expectations and definitions of project success and failure by city leaders, rather than against abstract definitions of success and failure or ex post rationalizations.

Space must also be considered in the evaluation of a project's success. Public investment in development projects may not be—and probably is not—the most efficient use of society's resources. But within the jurisdictional authority of city governments, it might be the appropriate way to enhance the city's revenues and to address a tax-services imbalance. Further, public investment is not necessarily designed to enhance the workings of the local marketplace or to generate a positive return on investment. The city's rationale for these actions may initially be the jobs and the capital investment that the project will generate; however, its long-term goal is more likely to be the enhancement of the tax base.

REDEFINING SUCCESS AND FAILURE

Given the contextual volatility of local economic development policymaking, local officials attempt to inject a degree of rationality into the decisionmaking process. They assess an array of conditions when they make decisions about whether the development projects they support have a good probability of succeeding. Nevertheless, this is not a study of successful or failed projects in a purely economic sense. Our focuses are how city officials select development tools for specific economic development projects, how they define success, and how they assess the city's monetary return on investment.

Stephen Linder and Guy Peters argue that "the empirical record of the successes and failures of a given instrument across problem situations becomes far less important than decisionmakers' perceptions of that performance."[3] We focus here on city leaders' perception of whether or not development projects achieved the goals they had for them. The portion of the interview dealing with project success began with the questions, What principal goals was the project designed to achieve? and How successful has the project been in generating revenues? The first question placed the issue of project success in the policymakers' political and economic setting and the second in the context of possible government failure. For the most part, local officials were remarkably candid in their assessment of a project's success.[4] Of the 40 projects examined, interview data and project files indicate that 27 were intended to generate revenue. Interview data, project files, and other documents allowed us to reconstruct the decisionmaking process fairly accurately.[5]

What follows is a systematic analysis of the salient characteristics of development tools and projects and their relation to success and failure. Local officials rely on a host of policy tools for the promotion of economic development. The characteristics of these policy tools are significant considerations in the decisionmaking process. But is there a pattern to these characteristics that can explain a project's success? Case-by-case analysis does not allow for the drawing of general conclusions; however, aggregate analysis does. Consequently, the remainder of this chapter aggregates the data from individual projects. This research approach has promise, because a separate decision was made for each development project about the kinds of tools selected, the scope of the city's investment, and the costs the city was willing to bear. Each project, then, represents a microcosm of how a city chooses certain development tools or a bundle of development tools.

The characteristics of development tools were grouped into four categories: resource intensiveness, political risk, constraint, and financial risk. Resource intensiveness refers to the administrative costs and operational simplicity of a given tool. Political risk involves the support of or opposition to a given tool. Constraint addresses the ideological acceptance of a tool. Financial risk is a measure of that risk to the city. We conceptualized these four categories in the following manner.

Resource intensiveness had two components: project complexity and project costliness. Complexity was based on the extent to which additional government resources were involved in the formulation and oversight phases of project development. Costliness was based on the actual annual per capita costs of city investment. This measure covered direct cash outlays from the city, and the value of in-kind contributions from the city (or forgone revenues). These costs represented direct or potential revenue loss to the city. Project costs did not include the total value of a bond issue but rather included the annual premiums as a means of calculating the annual city financial commitment to the project.[6]

Political risk also had two components: project visibility and its chance of failure. Visibility refers to the extent to which a project was publicly visible, that is, the position it occupied in public consciousness. The assignment of visibility values to specific projects was based on the level of media and public attention associated with the project prior to the project's approval. A low visibility project was one that received minimal media or public attention (based on the number and prominence of newspaper articles) and lack of written or oral objections to city officials that became part of the project file. A high visibility project received both extensive media attention and substantial written or oral objections. Moderate visibility projects possessed one of the two requisite characteristics. Chance of failure refers to the likelihood that a project would fail to accomplish what decisionmakers identified as its objective. The assignment of chance-of-failure values to specific projects resulted from documentation in individual project files (e.g., internal memoranda, testimony at public hearings) and assessments offered by interviewees on their a priori assessment of failure. Projects were assigned values based on the extent to which the prospects for breakdowns, bankruptcy, and bailouts were considered prior to the formal approval of the project.

Constraint also had two components: project intrusiveness and market signals. Intrusiveness is a measure of the ideological acceptability of a particular project. It was expected that, within a city, projects probably did not vary much on this dimension, especially if projects were initiated around the same time. These data were collected through interviews with city government officials and private sector leaders. Reliance on market signals or government was measured as the proportion of total public investment (federal, state, and local) to the total costs of a development project.

Financial risk gauged the risk of a particular development tool to the city's financial resources. Some of these tools require complex bond issuing regulations, others require simple cash transfers and minor infrastructure provision, still others result in legal entanglements. Inherent in each tool is a monetary or financial commitment of city revenues. (Chapter 4 describes how financial risk was determined.)

DEVELOPMENT PROJECT FINDINGS

The question, Did the project accomplish what it was intended to do at the time the project was initiated? focused on project success as defined in archival data and in interviews of city officials. The question, How successful has the project been in generating revenue? focused on project success in generating revenues for the city as defined in conventional return-on-investment terms. Below we analyze the answers to these questions, using the probit regression technique.[7]

Project Success

The first question we sought to address was whether any of the policy characteristics could predict project success as defined by city leaders. As the data in table 5.1 show, although the equation's chi-square significance levels and R-square indicate a good fit, the political risk variable (measured as the a priori chance of project failure) was the only characteristic with a statistically significant probit regression coefficient.[8] As the chances of failure increased during the planning, preapproval stages, the probability of eventual project success (defined in terms of achievement of stated objectives) decreased.

Knowing the political risk of a project aids in predicting the success of the project. In experimenting with interactive prediction, that is, altering the values of the independent variables to predict the dependent variable, the value of political risk consistently had the greatest impact. The coefficients are not directly interpretable as they are for ordinary least squares but have to be converted to probabilities. This process aids in estimating the probability of the dependent variable's occurrence given some values of the independent variable. A coefficient of 0, for example, means there is a 50 percent probability of the dependent variable's success. A probit coefficient of 1, however, corresponds to a probability of 84 percent that the dependent variable will be a success (conversely, a −1 corresponds to a 16 percent probability of success). For simulation purposes, we chose the mean value for each of the variables, save the political risk variable. It was allowed to vary from 1 to 3. The probability of success for a project whose political risk was rated 1 (low risk) is .99, while it is .35 for a project rated 3. This suggests that development projects rated average on five of six policy characteristics and rated 1 on the political risk variable will be considered successful by city leaders after the project is completed.

Projects in cities with poor economic health may not have achieved their stated objectives, while cities with robust economies could carry even the riskiest projects. To determine whether the crucial contextual variable of the city's fiscal and economic health was, in fact, producing the finding regarding political risk, an economic health variable was added to the model.[9] To capture the city's economic health, the UDAG distress measure (based on population growth, poverty level, income

Table 5.1

Six Characteristics of Development Tools and Prediction of Project Success

Variable	Six-Variable Model without Economic Distress			Six-Variable Model with Economic Distress		
	Coeff.	Probability	Mean	Coeff.	Probability	Mean
Project complexity	0.771	0.199	2.22	0.886	0.188	2.22
Project costliness	0.011	0.616	11.60	0.026	0.266	11.60
Political risk	-1.799	0.012	2.05	-2.142	0.017	2.05
Intrusiveness	0.257	0.756	1.43	0.608	0.526	1.43
Market signals	-0.331	0.277	2.92	-0.248	0.426	2.92
Financial risk	0.118	0.642	3.73	-0.125	0.675	3.73
Economic distress				-0.268	0.130	2.84
Constant	3.362	0.097		4.772	0.036	

Note: N = 37 development projects. Chi-square significance level = 0.0050 for model with no economic distress; 0.0035 for model with economic distress. Pseudo R-square = .334 for no economic distress; .364 for economic distress.

growth, unemployment rate, and job lag) was used. A score of o indicated very low economic stress, a 7 meant very high stress. Adding the contextual variable further underscored the importance of political risk but did not improve the explanatory power of the model. Local economic health seemed not to be related to project success. Despite the addition of this variable, political risk continued to dominate the model. The stable relationship between political risk and project success is noteworthy.

Two policy implications can be derived from these findings. First, there may be a meaningful lesson for city officials to draw about politically risky projects. The more controversial the project, the more likely the project will be unsuccessful, that is, that the public will react. The public is aware of unleased office buildings, plants operating at half capacity, convention centers without events, and vacant parking garages. If controversy surrounds a project's proposal, city leaders may want to think twice about committing city funds to it. Nevertheless, even in an economically troubled city, success can occur so long as it generates political support or if political controversy is muted.

Second, the unimportance of other policy characteristics that logically might affect project success is instructive. Analysis of the data suggests that the financial aspects of a development project—its costliness to the city, the risk to city funds, and the proportionate share of project costs borne by government—are less important than one might anticipate. Cost, financial risk, government share—these characteristics yielded no patterned relations with project success. The lesson for city leaders may be that they have substantial leeway in financing a development project that at the time it is proposed has a minimal chance of failing or arouses minimal political controversy. But if a project is highly visible and politically volatile, government investment is not likely to rescue it.

Evidence from specific cities underscores the preliminary finding that the perceived chance of failure during the planning phase predicts project success. For example, in Beaumont, the unofficial city policy is to contribute from city sources no more than 10 percent of the total cost for privately developed projects. Yet for the conversion of the Stedman Fruit Warehouse into an office and retail facility, the city exceeded the 10 percent limit. While the financial risks were relatively low—the developers were local and could be expected to deliver (in fact, the facility was 80 percent preleased before the developers approached the city for financial support)—the political risk was high. The city's official expectation for the project (and the reason they were willing to exceed their investment limit) was that it would leverage additional investment in the central business district. As city officials acknowledged, the project generated controversy because it exceeded standard investment practices. At the time of our fieldwork, the project had not leveraged additional investment and had not fulfilled its goals.

In Lowell, the city's efforts to encourage the refurbishing of abandoned textile mills enjoyed widespread popular and political support when it was announced. So when the owners of Wannalancit Mills requested a parking facility—without which, they claimed, further refurbishment would be impossible—the city obliged. As a consequence, Wannalancit invested millions of dollars more in the mill's rehabilitation. No real controversies arose over the proposed parking garage, and the project was successful in meeting its goal (textile mill conversion).

The revitalization of the Independence Square area of Independence was undertaken with an awareness of its political risks. Previous attempts to infuse the historic downtown with a redefined economic purpose had fallen short, even financially modest efforts. Some of the political risk stemmed from conflicting visions of the role of Independence Square. Ever since Kansas City displaced Independence as the dominant city in the region, Independence had been casting about for an economic identity. The consensus that something should be done was accompanied by skepticism that nothing would be successful. The city's annexation of outlying territory and the subsequent shift of residents and businesses to these distant areas further weakened Independence Square. Therefore, city-sponsored attempts to revitalize the area were hotly debated. The lack of success of the project is not surprising.

A politically popular and nearly risk free project occurred in Orlando. Skyrocketing demand for real estate and the concomitant high cost of housing made affordable housing scarce for the working poor. The city created a density bonus program that allowed developers to increase the number of multifamily residential units per acre if they contributed to the affordable housing program. The developer of the Wellington apartments took advantage of the policy by increasing housing density to 15 dwelling units per acre (over the allowable density of 12 dwelling units) and by contributing more than $58,000 to the Orlando Neighborhood Improvement Corporation, a low-income housing fund. In light of escalating housing costs, the project has enjoyed great political popularity.

Revenue Generation

The second question is more traditional in studies of economic development projects and asks whether policy characteristics can predict revenue-generating success, defined as city revenues from the project exceeding the public cost of the project. A dummy variable was used to code projects according to whether they actually generated positive net revenues or whether their return on investment was negative. Projects that were classified as development projects but were never intended to generate a profit or in which the linkage was tenuous at best (e.g., Huntsville's roadway project, Beaumont's Texas Energy Museum) were excluded from the analysis.

Because the dependent variable was dichotomous, probit regression again was utilized. As the data in table 5.2 suggest, no policy characteristic can be considered statistically significant in predicting revenue generation. Further, the significance levels for the chi-square statistic (.337) and the R-square statistic (.217) are both unacceptable. Adding the contextual variable of economic distress resulted in a statistically significant equation and a significant variable. Only the economic distress variable (and possibly the complexity variable) can be considered significant. These results indicate that projects located in economically healthy cities and, possibly, projects that are relatively routine (i.e., projects needing

Table 5.2

Six Characteristics of Development Tools
and Prediction of Revenue Generation

Variable	Six-Variable Model without Economic Distress			Six-Variable Model with Economic Distress		
	Coeff.	Probability	Mean	Coeff.	Probability	Mean
Project complexity	-0.464	0.280	2.22	-1.121	0.115	2.22
Project costliness	-0.014	0.428	9.65	0.047	0.292	9.65
Political risk	-0.240	0.485	2.04	-0.471	0.498	2.04
Intrusiveness	-0.057	0.945	1.44	-1.869	0.229	1.44
Market signals	0.091	0.707	2.89	-0.734	0.232	2.89
Financial risk	0.358	0.108	3.63	0.502	0.290	3.63
Economic distress				-1.363	0.089	3.15
Constant	-0.006	0.995		9.090	0.067	

Note: N = 27 development projects. Chi-square significance level = 0.3370 for model with no economic distress; 0.0009 for model with economic distress. Pseudo R-square = .217 for no economic distress; .476 for economic distress.

little oversight and start-up costs) are more likely to generate positive net revenues than projects with considerable overhead and start-up costs in economically distressed cities. To illustrate the predictive power of the economic distress variable on project revenue generation, consider a project with average ratings on all six variables but not on the economic distress variable. If the city within which the project is located is rated 4 (the median value) on the seven-point UDAG scale, the probability of generating net revenues to the city is virtually nonexistent (.009), while a score of 1 (extremely low distress) results in a .96 probability of net revenue-generating success. Varying only the complexity variable along with the economic distress variable slightly adjusts the probability of net positive revenues to the city, increasing to .999 the probability of revenue-generating success for projects that are routine and located in economically healthy cities and improving the probability of success to .16 in cities with a 4 rating on the economic distress variable.

Two policy implications might be derived from the preliminary analyses on revenue-generating success. First, city officials located in cities experiencing economic difficulties should probably not pursue development projects if their intentions are that the project generate a profit. The underlying strength of a region's economy is a fairly good predictor of a project's likelihood of generating a positive return on investment. Second, the possible significance of the complexity variable suggests that city officials should probably not patch together a complex assortment of development tools, although this implication is more tenuous than the first. At any rate, the complexity of the package may not have much impact on revenue-generating success. A city that offers more than its standard package of incentives for a project, especially one that requires greater-than-normal oversight or start-up costs, is likely not to see a financial gain from the project.

An important revenue generator for Orlando, for example, is the city's density bonus program. Orlando has experienced enormous growth since 1970, and its UDAG distress rating is 1—extremely low. Developers are permitted to increase housing density by up to 25 percent if they contribute to a low-income housing fund. The Wellington apartments resulted not only in a profit to the city's housing fund but also in higher property taxes from the multifamily residential units. Little oversight and no start-up costs kept the city's investment at a minimum.

Similar patterns can be discerned in other cities. Santa Barbara was able to manage its improvements to Lower State Street through its Community Development Office and to fund the project with tax allocation (or TIF) notes. The city intended its investment in streetscaping and parking facilities to stimulate improvements by property owners. Once this occurred, so the reasoning went, low-yield enterprises would be replaced by higher-yield ones, thereby increasing city revenues. This strategically important part of the central business district began to provide a return on the investment immediately after the improvements were completed.

At the other end of the spectrum is the economically depressed city of Springfield. In acute economic decline, this city embarked on an ambitious downtown revitalization plan that included restoration of the City Market building, realignment of railroad tracks, expansion of public parking, and rebuilding an Arcade (later, a hotel). Although the city's actual cash investment in the project was minimal, the coordination and oversight required was extensive. The implementation of this highly complex project did not proceed smoothly—in fact, the Arcade, which along with the City Market renovation was to be funded in part with UDAG money, folded, wreaking havoc not only on the project but also on the city's relation with the UDAG office in Washington. Although portions of the project were eventually completed, the City Market did not generate the expected revenues. In a city like Springfield, revenue-generating projects are desperately needed but, given the depressing economic environment, difficult to come by.

CONCLUDING OBSERVATIONS

Because markets, defined broadly and abstractly, have not failed, informed advice would recommend avoidance of government intervention in development projects because they probably would not enhance the efficient working of markets. Yet, the overwhelming evidence from our examination of public investment in development projects suggests that either market failure needs to be more broadly defined or government officials are irrational.[10] The former explanation is persuasive. The standard notions of market failure that might guide local government behavior omit the relevant issues of space and jurisdiction. That city investment is preferred by policy officials rests on the rationale that development incentives are not contestable in city markets and, indeed, that they can influence market efficiency. Development projects whose investment capital is insufficient require such city intervention.

Empirical data on project success and failure bring the market and government failure theories to the level of specific projects. Based on data from the projects, the preliminary lesson for development projects designed or supported because of their revenue-generating potential appears to be fairly orthodox, albeit with a slight twist. The orthodoxy is that the city's economic condition (measured by the city's economic distress) is an important predictor of the revenue-generating success of a project. The more healthy the city's economy, the more likely a profit will be realized from the city's investment. Officials in economically distressed cities would be ill advised to invest in projects for the purpose of generating a profit. Further, although innovative finance seems to enjoy great popularity among city development finance experts, the results from these projects suggest that the less complicated and the more routine or standard the incentives offered (especially by economically healthy cities), the greater the probability of revenue-generating success—although the significance level of .115 certainly tempers this inference.

In making decisions about which projects to support and how to support them, local officials need to calculate the degree of political risk in the project. It alone speaks volumes about project success, as measured by the perceptions of local officials. Although the data indicate that city governments support both low-risk and high-risk projects, city officials should mobilize public capital only for projects that enjoy wide local support. City leaders should gauge public apprehension about development projects and postpone or halt funding for projects that generate political conflict and controversy.

6 / URBAN OUTCOMES

THE OFFERING OF development incentives by city leaders is seldom a random process, as the evidence from the study cities confirms. Rather, incentives are provided for a purpose—the purpose of effecting change. How that change manifests itself is dependent upon the vision and dreams of city officials. City governments pursue development in the expectation that patterns of urban development will be altered in consonance with city officials' mental pictures of the good society.[1] To pursue development—and it is hoped achieve the vision—city officials mobilize public capital.

THREE INTERRELATED DEVELOPMENT OUTCOMES

As we argue throughout the book, the mobilization of public capital is a purposive activity in which a development project is undertaken with the expectation that it will generate desirable consequences or outcomes. Disneyland, according to John Findlay's account of future urban landscapes, possesses "magical" qualities "that exerted a powerful influence on urban form" around the country.[2] Those qualities are what cities pursue. City officials are not interested in converting their town into a massive amusement park governed by a large mouse but rather in capturing Disneyland's spirit and design. Other, more traditional, outcomes include enhancing the quality of life, improving employment and income prospects, stabilizing the tax base, rationalizing land use, enhancing the city's aesthetics, providing a sign of an economically healthy city, and symbolizing the "new" city.[3]

The outcomes of development projects influence the pattern of urban development that will (or has) come to characterize the city. This pattern of development, as defined in this chapter, has little to do with the city's profitability (or rate of return) from a project or with the efficiency of the project. Rather, it refers to how well city officials' visions match reality. The razing of a blighted area near downtown Seattle had little to do with renovating the city's central business district; the Seattle Center borrowed from suburban development patterns.[4] The evolution of Silicon Valley was rooted in providing a campuslike atmosphere for the nascent computer industry. The Galleria area in Houston symbolizes the triumph of wealthy, homogeneous suburbs.[5] The employee-owned steel mills of the Weirton Steel Company in Weirton, West Virginia, reflect the city residents' resolve to maintain that city's dominant physical structure.[6] Every city can point to some tangible results of an earlier vision; the most salient of which can be collapsed under three broad headings: (1) an increase in private *capital investment and property values* for the project area and for the area immediately surrounding the project, (2) an alteration in the *vista or physical appearance* of the project area or city, and (3) a shift in the *class of user* in the project area.

Although these three outcomes are identifiable, they are not automatically separable. Increased investment in a project area frequently changes both the vista and the class of user. However, despite the linked nature of the outcomes, they are based on different assumptions. And while project sponsors and promoters may cite all three in their defense of government investment, public discussion of the project eventually converges around a single preferred outcome.

Capital Investment and Property Values

One expectation of government-supported development projects is an increase in capital investment and property values at the project sites. These impacts are not necessarily limited to the project sites, however. One manifestation of development patterns is the resulting change in capital investment and property values in the surrounding, nonproject areas. Successful development projects often stimulate investment in and raise the value of adjoining property which, in turn, alters land use and subsequent development patterns. An important consideration in siting public facilities, such as monuments, museums, and parking garages, is the effect the facility will have on proximate properties, both commercial and residential. Knowledge (or presumptions) of these impacts may influence the political parameters within which capital mobilization decisions are made.[7] The same is true for publicly assisted, private development projects. A city may assemble a land package or make infrastructure improvements or arrange financing at a particular site because of the potential private investment in nearby sites.

In fact, it is in anticipation of positive spin-offs that a city government is often willing to support risky development projects, that is, those in which the direct return from the supported project itself is likely to be negative. This has certainly been the case with sports stadium construction. Even in the face of compelling evidence that constructing and operating major sports stadiums tends to drain revenue from cities, government investment is supported because of the purported multiplier effects.[8]

Since the property tax is a primary revenue source for city government, increased property values from proximate areas to the development project should yield increased property tax revenues to the city.[9] Even if a city provides property tax deferral or abatement for the project, investment in adjacent parcels will generate revenues. In fact, the revenue potential of nearby, nonproject sites weighs heavily in a city's calculation of the relative costs and benefits of its investment in a project. Such extension of capital investment and increased valuation can provide a fiscal shot in the arm to an ailing city and may bolster the tax-services balance in a prosperous city. In both types of cities, positive revenue streams enhance the political fortunes of elected officials.[10]

Vista or Physical Appearance

A second kind of development outcome is the alteration of the vista or physical appearance of the urban setting. Skyscrapers and sprawling buildings are another consequence not only of developers' and city officials' dreams but also of city-provided development programs. For example, government policies continue to be pursued that transform older downtowns into modern corporate office centers, upscale commercial establishments and residences, and hotels and other tourism-convention facilities.[11] Although some of the revitalization is adaptive reuse of existing space, much of it occurs in low-density areas. Thus a city takes on a different appearance as the result of the mobilization of public capital.

In 1868 an *Atlantic Monthly* reporter commented that Pittsburgh was "hell with its lid off."[12] The industrial revolution of that era, and the rapid urbanization that accompanied it, made a mark that has taken years to erase. But new structural images replace the old ones, and Pittsburgh is now among the least smoggy and polluted of American cities. Akron's rubber factories have been replaced by high-technology industries, Chicago's stockyards have been replaced by the Sears Tower, Lowell's textile mills have been replaced by condominiums, computer software firms, and museums, the St. Louis Arch replaced slums, Atlanta's Peachtree Plaza replaced institutional segregation, and Disneyland replaced the pastoral serenity of orange groves in Anaheim.[13] To make Boston the city that it is today, "quaint, old-fashioned, often eccentric architectural designs and structural patterns that many people had always found so charming and so characteristic of the three-hundred-year-old city [were] wiped out in favor of a growing array of modernistic glass-and-steel skyscrapers."[14] In each of these instances, the transformation of the urban landscape represents the replacement of one set of values and expectations with another. As urban morphologists argue, the cityscape transmits signals about the society that created it; it is a text to be read.[15]

The urban renewal programs of the 1950s and 1960s replaced slums with residential and commercial enterprises, a process that Bernard Frieden and Lynne Sagalyn refer to as "sanitizing the city."[16] The redeveloped area, cleared of the vestiges of the past, has a different look and ambience—and city officials hope, a glowing economic future. As G. J. Ashworth and H. Voogd note, "the perception of cities, and the mental image held of them, become active components of economic success or failure."[17] Thus, public capital is mobilized in an effort to improve the vista or physical appearance of the city.

Class of User

Development not only changes the economic attractiveness and physical look of the city, it may also shift the use of land from one class of user to another.[18] For example, in Boston, in the view of one observer, urban renewal took "an approach to neighborhood conversion that emphasized real estate values and investment profits at the expense of the working classes and the poor."[19] Boston is by no means atypical. And while the excesses and biases of the 1960s urban renewal programs are well known, contemporary development efforts have similar outcomes. The use of public capital to encourage gentrification, for example, is intended to reverse the flow of middle- and upper-income households to the suburbs; the central city is to be repopulated with a different type of resident. The shift from one type of land use to another is proposed as a means to an end, not as an end in itself. City policies that promote gentrification, for example, are also expected to spawn consumers for the products and services of the commercial activity stimulated by government funds. Presumably, then, the city's investment in these commercial activities can, at least partially, be paid back. Moreover, such policies are intended to change the image of the city to conform to the new land-use plan.

Changes in the class of user are not limited to residential replacement. Commercial substitution also occurs. Redevelopment frequently means that low-end, "mom and pop" commercial ventures are displaced by high-end, corporate endeavors. In the case of Newark, public capital was mobilized in support of the conversion of "a landscape of forlorn, weedy Park-Fast-All-Day lots ringed in razor wire . . . boarded-up buildings and a doomed, gutted hotel" to the New Jersey Performing Arts Center.[20] The activity remains commercial, but the targeted population is vastly different. The public investment was substantial: $62.5 million from the state of New Jersey, $10 million from the city, and $1.2 million from the federal government. (Approximately $26.5 million in additional funds came from private contributors.) And a successful change in the class of user should go a long way in shifting the common public perception of the inner city, which in the early 1990s could be summed up in the warning, Lock Your Car Doors.

Another change in class of user involves the conversion of residential properties to higher-yield, nonresidential uses. The master plans of many American cities are predicated on strategic land-use and zoning changes. The redevelopment of downtown Atlanta, for example, hinged on zoning changes favorable to powerful commercial interests.[21] The pattern is not unique to Atlanta—it is frequently residential use that is rezoned. Not uncommonly, these alterations in land-use patterns generate public outcry and, on occasion, organized resistance, and elected officials find themselves weighing the conflicting interests.[22] In instances like these, the mobilization of public capital will reconstitute land-use patterns.

PROJECT OUTCOMES

The answers to two questions, What were the intended outcomes of the various development projects? and What have been the actual outcomes? gave us outcome-related data. The accompanying photographs demonstrate the impact of the projects, loosely categorized according to the primary outcomes intended by city officials. As is immediately apparent, intended outcomes may not square with actual outcomes and intended outcomes may span all three categories of outcomes. In addition, a host of unintended consequences frequently arose.

Capital Investment and Property Values

Duluth's Storefront Renovation

Duluth's storefront renovation program was a city-initiated and city-funded project (see figure 6.1). Prior to the inauguration of the renovation program in 1982, the majority of the downtown storefronts were grimy and dull, which city officials believed repelled potential shoppers. They decided to push for renovation, without the endorsement of downtown businesses, feeling there was aesthetic and economic value in an architecturally consistent downtown.

The downtown businesses had been built in the latter part of the 1800s and early 1900s, and city officials wanted to preserve these turn-of-the-century storefronts, renovating them according to the architectural style dominant at the time. Participating store owners selected architectural designs from a list approved by the architectural firm hired by the city, to ensure that the designs were consistent with the overall plan. They borrowed money from a fund created by Duluth's Business Development Office, a revolving loan funded by TIF revenues from the downtown TIF district. The fund financed up to 30 percent of the cost of renovation (up to $300,000), and the lending rate was a very attractive 3 percent. Funds were capitalized primarily from tax increments and deposited in the city's economic development fund. City officials hoped that the increased capital investment at strategically located storefronts would spur investment in adjacent properties and enhance the city's tax base.

Needless to say, attractive storefronts are not the only reason consumers might choose to shop in Duluth's downtown rather than at suburban malls, which is where the retail sector has been migrating. If the

Figure 6.1 Duluth's Storefront Renovation.

storefront renovation project can be credited with the entire increase in constant-dollar sales tax revenues between 1982 and 1987, there would still be a net cost to the city of $50,000. (Table 6.1 shows the 1978–88 tax revenues from the central business district.) However, if the total increase in constant dollar property tax revenues over the same time period can be ascribed to the storefront renovation program, then net benefits slightly exceeded $1 million. This latter assumption may not be as overgenerous as one might suspect; property values throughout the city declined in nominal dollars between 1982 and 1987, from $1.21 billion to $1.19 billion. Therefore, increases in downtown property values go against this trend. Although the

Table 6.1

Duluth's Central Business District:
Property Value, Property Tax, and Sales Tax, 1978–1988

Year	Property Value (millions of 1980 dollars)	Property Taxes (thousands of 1980 dollars)	Sales Taxes (thousands of 1980 dollars)
1978	36.48	2,044	
1979	39.50	2,210	
1980	38.70	2,301	
1981	38.59	2,210	1,082
1982	36.89	2,271	1,021
1983	37.80	2,404	1,069
1984	35.84	2,301	1,086
1985	36.37	2,429	1,073
1986	36.74	2,452	1,122
1987	35.39	2,475	1,184
1988	35.15	2,557	1,146

Source: Data from Duluth Finance Department and Treasurer's Office.

storefront renovation program might not be a financial success, it certainly might have contributed to stabilizing downtown property values.

Lowell's Wannalancit Mills Office and Technology Center

Wannalancit Mills in Lowell is a 400,000-square-foot textile mill built in the 1830s on the Northern Canal. Developers purchased it in 1982 and renovated much of the old structure for office space and research and development laboratories (see figure 6.2). The Wannalancit Office and Technology Center began leasing in 1983 and was approximately one-fourth occupied that year. The developers, however, felt they were losing the burgeoning high-technology business to the suburbs because of lack of parking near the Wannalancit Center. They estimated they needed one parking space per 1,000 square feet of office space and asked the city to build a parking garage. Furthermore, the exorbitant costs of rehabilitating a century-old mill exceeded the financial capacity of the developers. The city then applied for a UDAG to be loaned to the developer and to defray the construction costs of a 1,250-car parking garage.

In 1984 Lowell was awarded a $2.4-million UDAG; $700,000 came in the form of a grant for construction of the parking garage and the $1.7

Figure 6.2 Lowell's Wannalancit Mills Office and Technology Center.

million balance as a 3 percent loan to the developers. The state contributed $4.2 million from its off-street parking program, and the city issued a $2-million general obligation bond for the parking garage. In 1985, after the parking garage was finished, the occupancy rate of Wannalancit Mills was nearly 98 percent. But by 1989, 20 percent was vacant, because of the downturn in the high-technology industry and the subsequent bankruptcy of Wang (headquartered in Lowell).[23] Consequently, even though Wannalancit developers planned to increase capital investments in the mill and the surrounding area, costs clearly exceed benefits. Nevertheless, if Wannalancit could not have expanded its operations without the parking garage (as the developers claimed), renovation would not have been as extensive, and property tax revenues would have frozen at their 1984 (prerenovation) levels. Increases in property tax revenues, therefore, can be considered a direct benefit of the parking garage and subsequent renovation. The before and after difference in property taxes is $55,444 annually between 1986 and 1989. If the increased property taxes are compared to losses from the parking garage, costs still exceed benefits (measured in property tax revenues) by more than $200,000 annually.

Moreover, the Wannalancit Mills renovation project had only a minor effect on land-use and development patterns. The exterior structure of the mill was not altered, so no signs are visible from the outside. Inside the mill, however, are brick walls, circular wooden stairways, hardwood floors, and the classic beauty of a nineteenth-century building. Nevertheless, the pattern of urban development around Wannalancit Mills is basically unchanged, except for the numerous automobiles on the nearby city streets and the parking garage.

Springfield's City Market and Hotel

Springfield's City Market and hotel project (see figure 6.3) illustrates not only Springfield's financial limitations but also the problems that have beset this city since the 1970s and what happens when a city in acute economic decline assumes some risks—and loses.

Figure 6.3 Springfield's City Market.

The city's 1980 master plan focused efforts on redeveloping the central core of the city's central business district. The main block of this core was purchased by the city and a new City Hall was erected on the site, freeing up space in the adjacent City Market where city offices used to be housed. The master plan called for the renovation of both the City Market (for small businesses and boutiques) and another building. Over the course of the next decade, the renovation project for this building fell through and a hotel was built on the project site.

The master plan was premised on the belief that new building in the core block of the central business district would stimulate additional renovation projects near that block and attract shoppers downtown. City investment in the Arcade and later in the hotel and City Market was made not with the expectation of generating a direct profit but rather of stimulating renovation and new construction and retail sales in the central business district. In fact, neither happened. There have been no visible signs of renovated buildings in the adjacent area. Building permits for a one-block radius around the City Market have been almost nonexistent, according to city officials. Both indicators, therefore, suggest that any intended indirect benefits of the project in the form of private investment have not been forthcoming.

After the Arcade was razed in 1989, the hotel was built across the street. Consequently, the physical appearance of that section of the central business district has been enhanced nicely. But the long-awaited private capital reinvestment appears not to have been realized: building permits do not indicate any reinvestment in the immediate area of the project, downtown retail sales have not been robust, shoppers continue to patronize the malls in the outside area, and the financial future for Springfield's central business district continues to be discouraging.

Boise's Towne Square Mall

Boise city officials recognized that converting existing agriculturally zoned land to a 1.1-million-square-foot regional mall would have a positive effect on the city's tax base. After effectively keeping the lid on development for many years, public demand grew, and a host of firms submitted bids to develop a regional mall to be located along an interstate highway interchange. A Salt Lake City developer was selected and began an extensive process of negotiation and compromise with the city. The firm, accustomed to dealing with economically stressed cities, found Boise a hard bargainer, according to most reports. Having given its ap-

Figure 6.4 Boise's Towne Square Mall.

proval to the zoning change, the city was willing to give little else away. The new mall, called Towne Square, and the anticipated spin-off development, was to be a "revenue cow" for the city.

Public expenditures for Towne Square Mall (see figure 6.4) are difficult to trace; however it appears that approximately $2.4 million in federal, state, and highway district funds went into the project. Boise's role in the development of Towne Square, once city policy was changed to allow it to occur, was primarily regulatory. The city did not take any of the property for Towne Square. Sewers were already in place, the state (with 75% of the funds coming from the federal government) developed the arterial roads, and the Ada County Highway District supplied local street improvements. Planners estimated the probable spin-off effect and planned for another 1.1-million square feet of supplemental commercial development.

In 1980s America, large regional malls begat minimalls. Data from building permits filed with the city indicate that Towne Square Mall, a $32.3-million project, stimulated another $14 million in commercial development on adjacent parcels:

Home Club	$1,800,000
T. J. Maxx	1,957,999
Shopko	3,700,000
Toys "R" Us	1,533,000
Costco	2,300,000
Club Wholesale	1,500,000
Cineplex Theater Complex	1,387,000

In no instances were property tax breaks provided to developers. Commercial development is tightly regulated in the secondary regional activity area (defined as the half-mile radius around the mall site). To protect nearby residential areas, the city adopted ordinances defining allowable commerce in the Towne Square Mall periphery. For example, the city encourages the consolidation of land into large parcels (approximately three or more acres) and specifically discourages strip development. In addition, planned development applications are required, and those proposals with mixed-use components are favored.

Towne Square Mall and the surrounding development has had a dramatic impact on Boise, with $46 million of commercial development replacing 170 acres zoned for agriculture. A retail explosion has occurred. Boise has successfully captured retail dollars that previously were lost to Salt Lake City or Spokane. And although the city of Boise does not benefit directly from the increased sales tax revenue (there is no point-of-origin mechanism in Idaho's sales tax), the property tax yield has increased exponentially. On the flip side, of course, are the negative externalities, such as traffic congestion and increased demand for public services. However, since traffic problems fall to the Ada County Highway District, increased demands can be covered by the enhanced revenue base.

Vista or Physical Appearance

Duluth's Fond-du-Luth Casino

The Fond-du-Luth Casino (see figure 6.5) was designed to attract tourists and give new life to the east end of Duluth's central business district. However, the city initiated the project only after it failed to convince the former owner of the building (Sears) to remain. The city wanted to ensure that the building did not remain vacant and that that section of downtown not be stigmatized by a grim view of boarded-up buildings

Figure 6.5 Duluth's Fond-du-Luth Casino.

and adult entertainment shops, which by the early to mid-1980s were beginning to characterize the area.

Duluth's investment in a casino required the city to pursue an exceptionally novel approach to development, even though it did not generate a profit by the time it was expected to. The city deeded to a Chippewa Indian tribe, the Fond du Lac band, land formerly occupied by the downtown Sears building. The band bought the building and renovated the first floor as a gambling casino, agreeing to create a joint city-band gaming commission to act as the governing board for the casino. The commission comprises four band members and three city-appointed members. The agreement also called for the city to raze adjacent buildings, which housed primarily adult entertainment stores, and to build a parking garage to serve the casino. The loan for the parking garage is being repaid by the commission from casino profits—and by the band's taxing power on its nearby reservation, in case the casino's revenues are insufficient. Under the terms of the contract, Duluth receives 24.5 percent of net proceeds and the band 25.5 percent. The remaining 50 percent is retained by the commission for other economic development projects and is insulated from the city's general fund revenues.

The casino is perceived as an important commercial anchor for the east end of the city. Indeed, small businesses and local artists have begun to move into the area immediately surrounding the casino project; these activities conveyed the "right" image for tourism and retailing, and private investment in the area picked up. Building permits for the area within two blocks of the casino in the two years prior to the opening of the casino were valued at $92,500. In the two years after its opening in 1986, the value shot up to $165,000. (These figures exclude renovation to the old Sears building for the casino and construction of the parking garage.) It is probable that this near doubling of private renovation investment can be attributed to the casino project. What is remarkable about the growth is that it was realized before the casino generated the expected tourism and gambling trade.

Both the city's image and its prospects for a healthy financial return appear to have been realized. The casino project was designed to stimulate tourism and also to enhance the image and attractiveness of properties around the development site, which is located on the fringes of the downtown business district. Once known as the porno shop strip, those businesses were closed and a parking garage built in their stead to service the project. The casino did not generate the tourism or the revenues the city hoped for when it wanted (initially, 1988 was to be a profitable year; it wasn't), but the image surrounding the area is no longer offensive to public officials. By 1991, the casino was reaping over $32 million in profits.[24]

Lowell's Eastern Canal Park
(Jack Kerouac Commemorative Park)

Lowell's Eastern Canal Park (see figure 6.6) was begun in 1985 with no city participation; when it was finished in 1988, it had cost the city of Lowell $2.5 million. Massachusetts was developing what it called a Heritage Park system, in which cities highlight their heritage. Lowell's heritage, the genesis of the American industrial revolution, was its textile mills, which were made possible by the diversion of rivers into miles of canals. Eastern Canal Park is supplemented by a park that highlights Lowell's textile mills, the first urban park operated by the National Park Service.

The city encouraged the conversion of the old textile mills to residential or business use (preferably high-technology enterprises), thereby maintaining the low-skyline of the city—none of the textile mills, nearly 100–150 years old, was taller than five stories. The city also decided that many of the mills should be razed to provide open space, especially if conversion created residential areas. Heritage Park system funds allowed the city to create open space and thus allow for the retrofitting of Massachusetts

Figure 6.6 Lowell's Eastern Canal Park (Jack Kerouac Commemorative Park).

Mills into condominiums: the view from the condominiums crosses the canal and includes Eastern Canal Park and the terminus of the rebuilt trolley line.

The area's skyline is still dominated by the old textile mills; the only new buildings are the Wang Training Center and the Hilton Hotel, and they are no taller than adjacent buildings. Thus the Canal Park affected the visual image of the city by opening up space near the mill area and also by inducing the renovation of Massachusetts Mills. In that sense, the project's effects on urban development patterns are significant.

Boise's Downtown Core

The downtown core of Boise is an eight-block area that forms the center of the city of Boise (see figures 6.7 and 6.8). In the mid-1960s, as part of a twelve-block urban renewal effort, the Boise Redevelopment Agency acquired the area and razed much of it. These actions had a chilling effect on the central business district. A group of architects and planners concluded in 1985 that "over the last 20 years it has been left to

Figure 6.7 Boise's Downtown before Development.

Figure 6.8 Boise's Downtown after Development.

dwindle and decay, and now lacks not only the physical construction of a vital CBD, but also the city life and spirit."[25]

In 1985, the Redevelopment Agency produced a new mixed-use plan for the district. The eight-block core was to include a convention center, a hotel, office space, retail shops, entertainment facilities, parking, a pedestrian mall, and a public plaza. But the years of stagnation had generated substantial public skepticism, so the first task was to get something—anything—moving. In a break with tradition, it was the city government that picked up the gauntlet. The new mayor committed $250,000 to the development of a public plaza, called the Grove, at the intersection of four blocks. And to engage the skeptical public, the city orchestrated a brick donation program whereby Boiseans could purchase a brick ($20 each) with their name inscribed on it for placement in the Grove. More than 13,000 bricks were donated. As this was occurring, the agency requested proposals from developers to develop any or all of the eight-block area. The southern half of the area had been cleared; the northern half had underutilized or vacant structures on it, six of which were Historic Register properties.

The Grove was dedicated in December 1986. The public plaza cost an estimated $1 million, with the Redevelopment Agency using federal funds to supplement the city's allocation and the brick donation program. Its job was to finance the construction of parking garages and streetscaping (planting trees, installing period streetlights, and building brick sidewalks, benches, and planters) in the downtown core. The agency used $12 million in federal funds and property tax revenues generated by the newly created TIF district (TIF funds are an increasingly important revenue source). Property values, a low $1.1 million in 1987 (the first TIF year), were expected to rise to $23.2 million by 1989.

Since 1985, the value of the eight-block area has increased greatly. In addition to the Grove, two publicly owned projects were completed and, at the time of this study, two were under way. In addition, the Greater Boise Auditorium District began construction of its convention center, using a 4.5 percent local option accommodations tax to fund the $9-million facility on land contributed by the Redevelopment Agency.

Five major privately funded projects were approved by the agency, four are completed. The land was priced according to a formula that takes into account development costs and an "appropriate" profit for the developer, given the local market. Developers were given long-term ground leases based on the calculation. An 11-story bank building, with a market valuation of $16.2 million, was constructed on the block west of the Grove. Two retail renovations, each with an estimated market valuation of $1 million, and a new $2.5-million retail center had been completed. Under way was a $3-million renovation of a historic property into office, retail, and residential use. Now, the property is on the tax rolls, and Boise's downtown is alive again. After years of stagnation, downtown Boise is harvesting economic gain. But, equally as important to leading Boiseans was changing the appearance and ambience of downtown Boise.

Independence's Independence Square

"If the street is a direction that links points in space, then the square is the most important point. The square also represents the most important aspirations of society, demonstrating the spirit, culture and potential of the city community."[26] Those words, written by a professor of architecture, have been embraced by city leaders in Independence. Historically, Independence Square has served as the focal point of the city. It has been a trading center where wagonloads of pioneers began their westward journey; it has been the site of slave auctions and a Civil War battle. Jackson County Courthouse, where former President Harry S. Truman began his political career as a judge in the 1920s, remains the dominant edifice on the square. The 20-block area's contemporary incarnation is as a commercial center, housing approximately 150 shops and professional services (see figure 6.9).

Independence is a maintenance city, one that has a relatively self-contained orbit and invests little public capital in economic development. However, given the importance of Independence Square to the community's self-concept, the city has repeatedly taken actions on its behalf. The motivation is always the same: to retain the vibrance of the square. In the 1980s, the city began to promote tours of historic sites in the area around the square, so city officials wanted it to be beautiful, quaint, and charming. To achieve that, the city moved in two directions. In 1985–86, Independence Square was defined as a redevelopment area under Missouri Statute 353, which provides property tax abatement on improvements or new construction for a 10-year period; for the following 15 years, the tax rate was to be 50 percent of the reappraised value. A redevelopment corporation was formed, and grand plans for importing a Chicago firm to redevelop the entire square were leaked to the press. The grand plans, unsurprisingly, fell by the wayside, and instead piecemeal redevelopment has occurred. (Limiting the redevelopment corporation's

Figure 6.9 Independence's Independence Square.

impact is the fact that it does not possess eminent domain power; the city council retained it.)

The other direction in which the city has moved is with a program of refurbishing the square, meaning removing some of the "improvements" undertaken in a former urban renewal program and returning the historic "feel" to the area. This program is funded primarily through CDBG funds. The city has planted trees, improved sidewalks, installed period street lighting, and enhanced building facades. While these improvements are expected to secure the square's economic base, they are even more important to the city in the creation of a historic vista.

Tourism, as measured by number of visitors and estimates of their spending, has benefited Independence. However as significant as the square is to Independence's psyche, it is a related development project that will likely determine its success. Between the square and the National Trails Frontier Center, the newest of Independence's tourist attractions, is a deteriorating nine-block area that the city is interested in redeveloping with tourist-oriented facilities. One concern is that the area's run-down look and hodgepodge of uses has a negative impact on the city's tourism potential. The city proposed the creation of a TIF district to redevelop the area known as South Square. However, in 1990, the city concluded that the substantial presence of nontaxable properties in the district would reduce the TIF yield below an acceptable point. Consequently, the city is shifting some of its CDBG funds to the south square area.

Class of User

Evansville's Walnut Centre

The pattern of urban development in Evansville has unfolded over the latter half of the twentieth century in a hub and spoke pattern. The Walnut Centre redevelopment area is located at the hub, the heart of the city's central business district. The purposes of the Walnut Centre project were to provide commercial and industrial space (it was rezoned M-1, a light industrial classification, from a mixed residential-commercial classification) close to the central business district, to raze substandard housing, and to improve employment and tax revenues in the area. Rather than raze all the structures at one time, the city decided to proceed in four phases. The third phase was completed in early 1989 (see figures 6.10 and 6.11).

The city financed the acquisition and razing of the homes, relocated residents, and in some cases built homes for them and consolidated lots for developers with $2.3 million of CDBG funds. Properties were consolidated and resold by the Evansville Redevelopment Commission, with proceeds being returned to the city's CDBG program for reprogramming. In addition to the CDBG funds, the commission issued a $2.3-million redevelopment bond (in reality, a general obligation bond), which financed the commission's activities. Nearly $27 million of private funds were invested between 1982, the initial year of the project, and 1989. The largest investment was made by the Evansville Printing Company (co-owned by the two local papers, the *Evansville Press* and the *Evansville Courier*), and groundbreaking started in early 1989 for the $15-million facility.

The principal purpose of the project was to change land-use patterns and thus revitalize an area of the city located next to the central business district. Two measures of revitalization—changes in tax revenues and changes in property values—demonstrate important shifts attributable to the Walnut Centre rezoning. Annual gross tax revenues (for all local governments) for phase-one properties totaled $14,002 prior to revitalization;

Figure 6.10 Evansville's Walnut Centre Area before Development.

Figure 6.11 Evansville's Walnut Centre Area after Development.

after the structures were razed and new businesses built, annual gross property tax revenues amounted to $22,480, a net increase of $8,478. This increase does not include the value of the Veterans Administration building, completed in 1987, which is tax-exempt property (construction costs were $3.3 million), nor does it include the Metropolitan Evansville Transit System's headquarters building, also tax exempt (construction costs were $2.5 million). Annual gross property taxes for phases two and three increased by $16,767.

For the nine years prior to the Walnut Centre's development, the average annual constant dollar value for building permits for renovation and construction in the Walnut Centre area was $57,457. After phase one began in 1983, the average annual constant dollar value over the next six years soared to $630,799. The 12-fold increase clearly can be attributed to the city's investment in the redevelopment project. (The value of building permits during 1973–88 is displayed in table 6.2.)

Table 6.2

Value of Building Permits for Evansville's Walnut Centre Area
(constant 1980 dollars)

Year	Value of Building Permits
1973	147,309
1974	8,361
1975	1,531
1976	30,246
1977	125,170
1978	141,414
1979	38,593
1980	12,900
1981	11,594
1982	21,008
1983	133,375
1984	218,080
1985	184,456
1986	820,962
1987	292,987
1988	2,134,937

Source: Evansville Building Commission files.

Lowell's Hilton Hotel Complex

In October 1979 Lowell started work on a master development plan that identified a hotel as one of the initial ten projects for the revitalization of its downtown area. These projects, including storefront renovation, were expected to cost nearly $160 million. The city and the Lowell Plan, Inc., formally approved the master plan in December 1980; the architects considered the downtown hotel to be the anchor of the downtown redevelopment efforts.

When the Marriott Hotel chain expressed an interest in building a hotel near Wang Laboratories on the outskirts of town, the city tried to convince the chain to build downtown because of the expected tourist trade resulting from an urban national park and because of the city's efforts to revitalize its downtown. Later, the Hilton Hotel chain replaced Marriott, which bowed out after several months of discussions. However, the downtown location did not pass several tests required by Hilton, including better street access, convenient parking, a convention center, and a major, dependable tenant (to guarantee occupancy much of the time). As a consequence, finances for the downtown hotel project now included a city-owned parking garage with 1,000 parking spaces, an access road from downtown to the interstate highway, restoration of the locks on the canals, renovation of Lowell Memorial Auditorium, and construction of the privately financed Wang Training Center adjacent to the hotel. In other words, a massive shift in land use was expected to reinvigorate the downtown business district. In 1983 HUD awarded Lowell a $5.6-million UDAG, $100,000 for administrative costs, $2.5 million as a loaned to Hilton (at 8 percent) to be repaid to the Lowell Development and Financial Corporation (LDFC); and $3 million as a grant to the city to build the parking garage.

Wang and the Hilton (see figure 6.12) opened in 1985 to rave reviews, but the celebration was premature, and the city soon found that the key public financing tool, the UDAG loan, was vulnerable to the business cycle of high-technology industries. According to a letter from the city manager to HUD dated March 1, 1988, a downturn in the high-technology economy worldwide between 1985 and 1987 hurt Wang and, as a consequence of its reliance on Wang, the Hilton. Actual revenues for the Hilton over its first three years of operation compared with projected revenues illustrate the hotel's financial problem and, by extension, the city's and LDFC's risk in loaning public (UDAG) funds to the Hilton:

Figure 6.12 Lowell's Hilton Hotel.

	1985	1986	1987
Projected revenues	$8.4 million	$11.9 million	$12.8 million
Actual revenues	6.0 million	9.7 million	9.0 million

Hilton stopped payments on the UDAG loan in February 1988, expecting to resume in January 1990. But in July 1990, the occupancy rate for the Hilton averaged only 50 percent, and the loan underwent foreclosure.[27]

City officials had expected that the hotel complex, including the parking garage, would stimulate development throughout the immediate area of the hotel. One means of measuring those benefits is to compare renovations and additions to properties within one block of the Hilton and directly across the Concord River before and after project construction began in 1984. The average annual value in building permits between 1974 and 1983 was $98,516 (constant dollars); if the first two years of the study period are left out because of their small value, that figure is $122,954 (1976–83). For the post-Hilton period, the average annual value in building permits is $199,402 (constant dollars); and if 1984—the major construction year for the hotel—is removed, the new figure is $265,869. Comparing the post-Hilton average of $265,869 with the pre-Hilton figure of $122,954 yields a margin of nearly $143,000 in annual improvements that conceivably could be attributed to the hotel complex. If 2.5 percent of each year's construction value is capitalized into ad valorem property tax revenues for the city, and if the post-Hilton project margin can be attributed fully to the project, then the Hilton project generates nearly $3,500 in city taxes each year—which reduces only marginally the $154,000 annual net cost of the project to the city.

Property tax revenues from the Hilton Hotel and the Wang Training Center should have covered all financial losses to the city for the first three years, but with the closing of the Hilton and the bankruptcy of Wang, the project is no longer a financial success. Nevertheless, the city's vision, as expressed in the master plan, of reinvigorating the downtown business district has come true at least partially. In the late 1980s, a fledgling nightlife and restaurant business emerged, altering land-use patterns—in part as a response to the hotel project. Probably the most evident visual modification of downtown Lowell is the two new multistory buildings (Wang and the Hilton) among the century-old textile mills and three-story, turn-of-the-century businesses. The refurbishing and renovation of nearby buildings also enhance the city's visual image.

Beaumont's Texas Energy Museum

The Texas Energy Museum in Beaumont—a history, science, and technology museum—is a key part of Beaumont's efforts to change the class of user in its downtown area (see figure 6.13). In the mid-1980s, a prominent Texas oilman was looking for a home for the oil-related museum his company had established at its Fort Worth headquarters. Beaumont became a logical site because the local state university, Lamar University, had the makings of its own oil museum with its Spindletop collection. Serendipitously, Lamar and the city had already agreed to renovate a building owned by the city in order to bring the university's collection to the downtown area. Lamar had committed $750,000 to the building's renovation. The city's financial commitment involved the provision of in-kind staff time and the building, which it had been using for storage. When last on the property tax rolls in the mid-1980s, the building had an appraised value of $279,600.

Local officials reacted swiftly and in a distinctively Beaumont manner to the opportunity to transform the Spindletop holdings into a full-fledged energy museum (along with the Ft. Worth collection, which was valued at $2 million). The mayor and the city manager, along with Lamar's president, created the Texas Energy Museum Foundation, a publicly sup-

Figure 6.13 Beaumont's Texas Energy Museum.

ported entity, and the Texas Energy Museum, Inc., a private foundation. The city spearheaded a fund-raising effort, which netted $1.1 million in pledges within weeks. In 1989, with renovation and expansion under way, it was estimated that the museum would need an additional $1.3 million to open its doors. The city government was not in a position to provide these funds, so the museum board redoubled its effort to secure additional private support. And while city officials have played prominent roles in the fund-raising process, city government has played a distinctly minor part. In keeping with its development ethos, city government focuses on appealing to private firms, individuals, and foundations.

The Texas Energy Museum is being marketed as another piece in Beaumont's cultural mosaic. It contributes to the city's efforts at economic diversification through tourism promotion. It is valued, too, for its contribution to the quality of life; amid one of the most industrialized communities in Texas, a city in which oil derricks and cargo ships figure prominently, the museum is a cultural oasis. Its location on the same double block as the Art Museum of Southeast Texas and adjacent to both the Tyrrell Historical Library (undergoing restoration in the late 1980s) and the Julie Rogers Theater, represents a cultural consolidation in the downtown area. Whether it will be successful in shifting the class of user remains to be seen.

Santa Barbara's La Colina Housing Project

Santa Barbara intended its development of 50 units of permanently affordable housing (see figure 6.14) on one of the last undeveloped parcels in the city to change the class of user from what would likely have resulted had it not intervened. What makes this case so interesting is that the city's action had the effect of lowering (in socioeconomic terms) the class of user. The undersupply of affordable housing has been repeatedly identified as a problem in the area. The city's cash investment, through its redevelopment agency, was approximately $720,000 of the $4.7-million project. In addition, a rezoning from single-family to multifamily residental was necessary. There was little questioning of the forgone property taxes associated with the decision to build affordable housing rather than allowing the marketplace to produce more expensive housing. In fact, the only negative sentiment came from the surrounding neighborhoods and centered on the project's effect on their property values.

In 1982, the city's Redevelopment Agency, using TIF funds, purchased the 8.61-acre tract for $560,000 and made $160,000 worth of improve-

Figure 6.14 Santa Barbara's La Colina Housing Project.

ments. Construction financing was provided by a local conventional lender. Most of the permanent financing was provided by the California Housing Finance Authority (whose funds are generated by tax-exempt bonds). The balance of permanent financing, approximately $672,000, was provided by the Redevelopment Agency. One-third of this amount were funds the agency had in land banks and public improvements; the remaining $450,000 was loaned by the agency to the Community Housing Corporation, a nonprofit housing development organization. Approximately $500,000 of CDBG funds were used for off-site improvements, including a storm drain and sewer line.

The city tightly controls La Colina and retains the authority to approve resale of the units for thirty years. The sales price is tied to the increase in the median income in the city. Two years after La Colina's completion, the price range of the units was $110,000 to $114,000. As with the original sale, new buyers must meet income limitations. The city intends that the units be permanently affordable, so an owner cannot take advantage of the rapidly escalating property values in the marketplace. Knowledgeable city officials estimate that area property values increased approximately 50 percent between 1986 and 1989, and that estimate probably holds true for the La Colina area. The project has not depressed the values of adjacent property; the neighborhood's housing price growth curve is markedly similar to that of the city as a whole. In fact, new market-rate housing is being constructed nearby.

In sum, public capital, in the form of rezoning and revenues generated by the city's TIF district, was mobilized for the La Colina housing project. The city initiated the project, invested in it, and changed the class of user from what the market would have produced. Given the local economy and the city's explicit commitment to increasing the affordable housing stock, the city's investment is secure, both economically and politically.

CONCLUDING OBSERVATIONS

In comparing the findings across the 12 projects, the difficulty in separating one intent from another or one outcome from another is apparent. Even in communities with widespread consensus regarding public capital mobilization, projects frequently carry multiple intents. The outcomes are interconnected—the data make it clear just how interrelated. What

Table 6.3

Intents and Outcomes of the 12 Development Projects

Project	Increased Capital Investment and Property Values	Improved Physical Appearance	Change in Class of User
Capital investment intent			
Duluth's storefront renovation	?	+	
Lowell's Wannalancit Mills	−	−	
Springfield's City Market	−	−	
Boise's Towne Square Mall	+	+	+
Physical appearance intent			
Duluth's Fond du Luth casino	+	+	+
Lowell's Kerouac Park	+	+	+
Boise's downtown redevelopment	+	+	+
Independence Square	?	+	
Class of user intent			
Evansville's Walnut Centre	+	+	+
Lowell's Hilton Hotel	+/−	+	+
Beaumont's Texas Energy Museum		+	?
Santa Barbara's La Colina housing		+	+

Note: + Indicates intent realized (as of 1990). − Indicates intent not realized. ? Indicates uncertainty regarding outcome. A blank means no intent, no outcome.

is especially interesting, however, is that projects frequently produce unanticipated outcomes.

The Lowell Plan, for example, envisioned a revitalized central business district anchored by a major hotel, and prior to 1987, the city's return on its investment was positive. Later, however, it was not. But even though the economic fortunes of the city that was brought to the public's imagination as the Massachusetts Miracle town have plummeted since the mid-1980s and the project can no longer be considered a financial success, the Hilton project's secondary purpose was achieved. The physical appearance of downtown Lowell has been altered substantially. In the midst of a grimy mill town, new buildings were constructed and, for a while, private investment in surrounding buildings surged.

Not all vistas or users change according to plans. And return on investment is not always good or even positive. Developers' plans to build a mall on or near the Manassas, Virginia, Civil War battlefield, which would change forever the look and feel of the historic site, failed because of public opposition.[28] In many cities, vacant lots symbolize the failed dreams of architects of the urban landscape. Many downtown festival markets that opened to rave reviews are beginning to falter.

In the cases we examine here, there appear to be primary intents and primary outcomes as well as secondary, yet important, outcomes. Table 6.3 summarizes the intents and outcomes of the 12 projects. Measured against their objectives, not all projects' outcomes can be classified as successful, but nearly each one altered some aspect of the city's image, for better or worse.

7 / ON POLITICS, MARKETS, AND IMAGES

CITIES ARE dynamic places, constantly evolving. The old city reconfigures itself as a new and (perhaps) different place. Throughout this process, the very visible hand of city government is at work. However, while city government controls land (or space), it has little control over labor or capital. It is the interaction of politics and economics that produces the cityscapes of the next millennium.

The spatial implications of private capital investment decisions and individual decisions to migrate are not the only, and probably not the most important, determinants of the form and structure of a city. Instead, it is government promotion of urban economic development projects that most profoundly alters a city's landscape; the critical elements in transforming the extant urban landscape into the cityscape of tomorrow are twofold: (1) the vision of a city's leaders, their determination and commitment to pursue their vision, and their capacity to mobilize public capital for the attainment of the vision and (2) the strengths, diversity, and resiliency of the local economic base. These elements determine whether a city is survivalist, expansionist, maintenance, or market oriented.

Much of the development literature of the 1980s marginalizes the actions of the public sector, especially localities. But city governments are central actors. Our argument is that the mobilization of public capital— or how local officials select, package, and utilize the policy instruments at their disposal—is primary. As the data regarding the cities in this study show, the behavior of local government varies from one place to another and, within a city, from one project to another. But it is never inconsequential; it matters. Steven Erie reminds us, with regard to Los Angeles, that "L.A.'s chief early asset was leadership . . . with plans for building a Great City. In the end it was public water . . . that built modern-day Los Angeles, underwrote its thriving real estate industry, and transformed it into an imperial city."[1]

DYNAMIC VISIONS AND ASPIRATIONS

The envisioned city of tomorrow is not static; it evolves in response to shifting economies and political coalitions. A city's underlying economic base, its governing coalition, and the vision of its leaders are in constant tension with other conflicting opportunities, possibilities, and visions. A change in city leadership and the governing elite, the closing or downsizing of a large firm, or a substantial change in state aid or unfunded mandates will, among other factors, influence the vision of the city's leaders and affect the underlying economy. These shifting influences are critical in the "creative destruction"[2] that alters the economic landscape and political aspirations and that ultimately changes the city's image and visions. Changes in vision and market adjustments in the economic base, then, profoundly affect a city's approach to economic development. The mobilization of public capital as a mechanism for achieving the vision may change as well.

With the defeat of political coalitions come new visions and images of the city. The old visions, dispatched to the dustbin of history, give way to the new order. When voters replaced Boise's leadership with more pro-active officials in the mid-1980s, a new vision was one of the most obvious results. The mayoral-led coalition talked in terms of regional prominence, and in hopes of achieving this prominence, boldly marshaled public capital in support of development projects. The kinds of development tools used by the city and the types of projects it sponsored were vastly different from those of the previous regime. In effect, Boise was transformed from a maintenance city to an expansionist city. Thus, the mayor's 1987–88 budget message was full of phrases like "first steps in a new direction" and "building the foundation of a new future." In the minds of local leaders, Boise will eventually rival Denver in terms of regional importance.

The shifting categories of the study cities from 1984 to 1992 are as follows:[3]

- Survivalist cities (high distress, high activism)

1984–86	1990–92
Duluth	Duluth
Evansville	Evansville
	Lowell

- Expansionist cities (low distress, high activism)

1984–86	1990–92
Huntsville	Huntsville
Lowell	Orlando
Orlando	Boise

- Market cities (high distress, low activism)

1984–86	1990–92
Beaumont	Beaumont
Springfield	Springfield

- Maintenance cities (low distress, low activism)

1984–86	1990–92
Boise	Santa Barbara
Santa Barbara	Independence
Independence	

A city's underlying economy influences city leaders' images and their perceptions of their city's prospects—which in turn may affect the way the city manages its economic development function. The bankruptcy of a large manufacturer, the shifting center of retail sales from old downtown department stores to suburban malls, the realignment of the domestic economy from an industrial to a service base, and other changes to a city's economic base influence not only the tax-services balance but also city leaders' perception of the city's relevant economic orbit.

Lowell, for example, became the showcase for Massachusetts's economic miracle of the 1980s. The refurbishment of the city's numerous abandoned textile mills, massive private investment in high-technology industries (especially Wang Industries), the promotion of grand public-private investment strategies, and the aggressive pursuit of federal grants all contributed to the city's rapid economic growth. The political leadership, as a consequence of this strong underlying economy, fashioned visions of a better, more vibrant Lowell. The city was encouraged to invest in development projects as a means of pursuing its vision to be a competitor city with other high-technology cities, not just the cities in its geographic region.

By the late 1980s and early 1990s, however, Lowell's economy, like that of Massachusetts and New England in general, began to falter. Unemployment rose, income stagnated, and by 1990 housing prices were down by 25 percent since 1986.[4] Most important to the city's economic misfortunes, Wang went bankrupt in September 1993 and reemerged as only a shadow of its former self.[5] The centerpiece of the Lowell Plan's revitalization of the downtown, the Hilton Hotel, filed for bankruptcy. (In the same week, the city's main downtown department store, Jordan Marsh, closed, in large part due to the opening of a Jordan Marsh branch as an anchor in a large mall 10 minutes away in New Hampshire, a state without a sales tax.) Lowell's aspiration of moving to a new plane, rapidly gave way in the early 1990s to a city trying to survive in the new economic order. Visions of competing with the Research Triangles and Silicon Valleys gave way to merely maintaining the city's position in its new orbit.

The economic foundations of cities change over time, changing their level of distress, which we used to classify the study cities. These changes in the relative strength of a city's underlying economy influence city leaders' aspirations. Public resources for development purposes will continue to be mobilized but for different objectives. In cities whose economic fortunes are declining, city leaders will mobilize public capital to recoup those losses, putting expansionist aspirations on the back burner until lost ground is made up. Lowell city leaders now see Lowell's competitors as cities in Massachusetts and New Hampshire, not those in the Silicon Valley and Research Triangle.[6] On the other hand, in those cities that have maintained their low-stress position, city leaders mobilize public capital either to sustain their city's position (Santa Barbara) or to move it to the next level (Orlando).

DEVELOPMENT PROJECTS: TENTATIVE LESSONS

A city's development function is promoted vigorously, we argue, in response to a tax-services imbalance or as a means of moving the city to a higher economic orbit. In the former case, the city wants to maintain its level of services by promoting development projects that eventually will recoup tax revenue losses or relieve strains on its service delivery functions. In the latter case, the city's interest is to expand its economic position vis-á-vis higher-order cities. In both cases, support of the city's economic development function is not necessarily viewed as an expansion of the city government's power. Rather, development is supported as the city's most effective mechanism for maintaining service delivery and for expanding services. Basic service provision is complemented by a healthy economic base, and development projects are designed, at least in part, to meet the city's service needs.

Regardless of design and intent, however, the data from the 10 study cities render some tentative observations about the efficacy of development projects. First, the underlying economic conditions of cities have a powerful effect on the revenue-generating potential of urban development programs—the poorer a city's economic health, the less likely a development project will generate a profit to the city. As a consequence, the city may not meet its objective of maintaining service levels. On the other hand, if a city's underlying economy is generally sound, the prospects of a positive return on investment are greater, and the fiscal capacity to fund more services or provide better services is enhanced. Moreover, there is some evidence that routine projects are often associated with profitable projects, while complex ones, those involving state or federal aid and city council approval, are less likely to be. The purpose of city investment can also be to promote an image of the city, to clear blighted areas, or to provide open space for aesthetic reasons. The data suggest that these projects are successful to the extent that there is a broad base of political support for the project; the more controversial the project at its initiation, the greater the probability it will later be deemed a failure. Political consensus needs to be established to reduce the controversy surrounding a development project.

Our observations are based on detailed analyses of 40 projects in 10 medium-sized cities. However, our four-celled matrix of city types covers all of the behavioral possibilities, so our findings are generalizable beyond the study cities. Anecdotal evidence suggests generalizability. A survivalist city, for example, expends public capital to secure its niche in the relevant system of cities. Early in 1994, a southeastern city that would be classified as survivalist in our framework mobilized $13 million in public funds (local, state, and federal) to attract a regional airline headquarters. The airline venture was risky, but in the words of a city councilmember, "We have to face the fact that we are in between [geographically] two competitive players. And if we don't compete, they will snuff us out."[7]

A CITY'S LIMITS

A city government's economic influence extends not far beyond its political boundaries. Perceptions of market failure by city officials, then, are tied spatially to the area over which they exercise control. Public intervention through a city's economic development function is an important tool in expanding a city's economy and encouraging its movement to another orbit in its system of cities, in reestablishing a tax-services equilibrium and improving the revenue profile, and in maintaining a city's status in its city hierarchy and regulating or managing its economic growth.

Politics matters in explaining the path and direction a city chooses, because local officials perceive a relevant orbit and then try to mobilize public capital in a manner intended to keep their city in (or move it to) that orbit. City officials may also choose to allow market forces to determine the city's orbit. In either case, market forces, a city's comparative advantage, the relative prices of land, labor, and capital—in short, the underlying local economy—influence these perceptions and the city's approach to development policy.

City political leaders' images of the good society and their perceptions of their city's relevant orbit are the political foundations for a city's economic development functions and for the political decision to mobilize public capital. Cities have different kinds of orbits: some are expanding, some are self-contained, others are relatively uncertain. Boise may never displace Denver; Orlando may achieve world class status; Springfield may fall to a lower plane; Huntsville may eclipse less-aggressive competitors. The choices made by the city government matter. City investment in, and regulation of, development projects is the most effective means by which a city controls and molds its growth, development, and pursuit of its future cityscape.

APPENDIXES

A / CITY POPULATION AND

LAND AREA

Table A.1

Population of the Study Cities, 1900–1990

City	1900	1910	1920	1930
Beaumont				
Population	9,427	20,640	40,422	57,732
Percentage change		+118.9	+95.8	+42.8
Boise				
Population	5,937	17,358	21,393	21,544
Percentage change		+191.4	+23.2	+0.7
Duluth				
Population	52,969	78,466	98,917	101,463
Percentage change		+48.1	+26.1	+2.6
Evansville				
Population	59,007	69,647	85,264	102,249
Percentage change		+18.0	+22.4	+19.9
Huntsville				
Population	8,068	7,611	8,018	11,554
Percentage change		-5.75	+5.3	+44.1
Independence				
Population	6,974	9,859	11,686	15,296
Percentage change		+41.4	+18.5	+30.9
Lowell				
Population	94,969	106,291	112,759	100,234
Percentage change		+11.9	+6.1	-11.1
Orlando				
Population	2,481	3,894	9,282	27,330
Percentage change		+57.0	+138.4	+194.4
Santa Barbara				
Population	6,787	11,659	19,441	33,613
Percentage change		+77.0	+66.7	+72.9
Springfield				
Population	38,253	46,921	60,840	68,743
Percentage change		+22.7	+29.7	+13.0

Source: *County and City Data Book (1983); 1970 Census of Population: Characteristics of the Population; 1990 Census of Population: Characteristics of the Population* (Washington, D.C.: Government Printing Office).

1940	1950	1960	1970	1980	1990
59,061	94,014	119,175	115,919	118,102	114,323
+2.3	+59.2	+26.8	-2.7	+0.5	-3.2
26,130	34,393	34,481	74,990	102,451	125,738
+21.3	+31.6	+0.3	+117.5	+36.6	+22.7
101,065	104,511	106,884	100,578	92,811	85,493
-0.4	+3.4	+2.3	-5.9	-7.7	-7.9
97,062	128,636	141,543	138,764	130,496	126,272
-5.1	+32.5	+10.0	-2.0	-6.0	-3.3
13,050	16,437	72,365	137,802	142,513	159,789
+12.9	+26.0	+340.3	+90.4	+2.3	+12.1
16,066	36,393	62,328	111,662	111,806	112,301
+5.0	+130.1	+68.6	+84.7	+0.2	+0.4
101,389	97,249	92,107	94,239	92,418	103,439
+1.2	-4.1	-5.3	+2.3	-1.95	+11.9
36,736	52,367	88,153	99,006	128,291	164,693
+34.4	+42.5	+68.3	+12.3	+29.6	+28.4
34,958	44,854	58,768	70,215	74,414	85,571
+4.0	+22.1	+31.0	+19.5	+6.0	+15.0
70,662	78,508	82,723	81,926	72,563	70,487
+2.8	+11.1	+5.4	-1.0	-11.4	-1.9

Table A.2

Land Area of the Study Cities, 1940–1990 (square miles)

City	1940	1950	1960	1970	1980	1990
Beaumont	10.4	31.4	70.8	71.6	72.9	80.1
Boise	5.1	6.8	10.3	23.4	39.3	46.1
Duluth	62.3	62.3	62.6	67.3	67.3	67.6
Evansville	9.7	18.0	32.0	36.0	37.3	40.7
Huntsville	a	a	50.7	109.1	113.5	164.4
Independence	a	10.0	13.8	47.8	80.6	78.2
Lowell	12.9	12.9	13.1	13.6	12.9	13.8
Orlando	10.5	14.1	21.1	27.5	39.5	67.3
Santa Barbara	15.4	16.8	19.7	21.0	18.7	18.9
Springfield	11.8	12.1	15.7	16.7	18.1	19.5

Source: *County and City Data Book* (Washington, D.C.: Government Printing Office, various years); *1990 Census of Population and Housing* (Washington, D.C.: Government Printing Office, 1990).

a. Not available.

B / THE DEVELOPMENT TOOLS

USED BY THE STUDY CITIES

BEAUMONT

Two categories of development tools are typical in Beaumont: tax incentives and loan programs. Beaumont has the authority to offer five-year property tax abatements for the construction of new manufacturing facilities or the expansion of existing plants. The abatement level is tied to the amount of capital invested or the number of full-time, permanent jobs created. For example, a project with capital costs ranging from $1 million to $2.5 million or one creating between 26 and 50 permanent jobs is eligible for a 25 percent reduction in property taxes.

Property tax abatement is available for residential or commercial buildings that are "historically significant sites in need of tax relief to encourage preservation." Once a qualified structure has been restored, it is taxed at its prepreservation assessed value for ten years.

Recent changes in Texas statutes have expanded the supply of development tools that have tax incentives as a primary component, so Beaumont can establish reinvestment zones for the purposes of tax-increment financing. In these zones, the additional property tax revenue generated by private development is used to finance the public improvements that made the new private development possible. The latest addition to development-promoting incentives is the state's enterprise zone program: the state selected 10 projects for enterprise zone status in 1988 and designates additional areas periodically. Firms located in an enterprise zone qualify for property tax abatement and refunds of state sales and use taxes on equipment and building materials. (Firms in a state enterprise zone must include among their employees a specified proportion of zone residents or economically disadvantaged individuals.)

Loan programs are also used in Beaumont. One new program is a loan pool that is essentially a coventure between local banks and investors. Called diversifinancing, the program is intended to provide low-cost capital for new or expanding business firms that create new jobs and broaden the economic base. The city encourages investors to buy two-year certificates of deposit (the amounts range from $25,000 to $100,000) that pay 4 percent interest (once the funds have been drawn for a loan). Banks pool the investments and make loans to qualified borrowers at 5.5 percent. The city's goal is a $10-million loan pool; a year after its inception, the program had attracted approximately $2 million in investments. Although the city has no direct financial involvement in the diversifinancing program, it actively promotes and markets the program to potential investors and borrowers.

Another loan program is the small business revolving loan program. The city uses CDBG funds to leverage private sector financing. (The ratio is $2 of private capital for every $1 from the program.) The program provides below-market rate financing for new or expanding businesses with fewer than 100 employees. The maximum loan amount is $100,000. The loan may be used for a variety of purposes, ranging from property acquisition and construction to equipment purchases and working capital. The purposes of the loan determine its rate and term. The expectation of the program is that every $10,000 invested will create one new job.

CDBG funds may be packaged in a variety of ways. For instance, the city can draw down its idle CDBG funds and loan them at below-market rates to developers whose projects primarily benefit low-to-moderate-income citizens. In the earliest years of private projects, Beaumont can guarantee debt service payments for developers seeking bank financing for projects intended to benefit low-to-moderate-income citizens. Through a nonprofit downtown development corporation, CDBG funds capitalize a revolving loan fund that is available for the rehabilitation of downtown structures. Public funding is matched by conventional bank financing. HUD loan guarantees are also available. Under this program, the city can use HUD funds for public improvements and land acquisition in support of job-creating private projects. The HUD funds are advanced to the city against its annual CDBG allocation.

Beaumont's development tools cost the city very little. None involve a direct expenditure by the city; instead, they involve the creative use of federal funds and a willingess to forgo property tax revenue.

BOISE

A 1982 study ranked Idaho dead last among the states in the degree of discretionary authority available to its local governments.[1] In addition, few development tools were available. The cost reduction incentives used by other study cities are unavailable to Boise. For example, prior to the Tax Reform Act of 1986, industrial revenue bonds were used as general development tools in many states. In Idaho, however, these bonds were restricted to industrial development facilities, warehousing, solid waste disposal, and ski areas. As a result, Boise could not use industrial bonds to leverage its burgeoning high-technology, research and development economy. In addition, property tax abatement, a staple of development in the Southeast, is illegal in Idaho. Boise, then, has to package the tools that it does have at its disposal in a creative manner.

Land use is a powerful tool in Boise. Although the city has not consciously pursued a policy of land acquisition, it has, through its Redevelopment Agency, engaged in limited land purchase and resale. The amount of property acquired has not been great; however its location in the central business district made it potentially valuable. The agency sells the property to a developer and builds public infrastructure, primarily streetscaping and parking. In addition, Boise has an urban homesteading program, in which housing that the city has acquired is made available to first-time home buyers through low-interest loans. The city also negotiates land exchanges, an especially useful tool for the city's development of its greenbelt. Through the program, the city swaps outer parcels for small strips of land along the river.

Besides a restrictive state government, Boise has to contend with government fragmentation in its metropolitan area. There are 40 local governments in the metropolitan area, three-quarters of them special districts. The Ada County Highway District controls the streets and sidewalks of the city. Independent sewer districts also exist. The city, therefore, does not hold all of the development cards. Infrastructure installation and improvements often depend on another unit of government.

The redevelopment of downtown Boise set the stage for an increase in the city's development tools. A tax increment financing law, passed especially for Boise in 1987, froze tax collections in an eight-block redevelopment area at their 1987 levels. Revenue from subsequent increases in value is diverted to the Redevelopment Agency. The affected taxing entities, such as the school district, the county, and the county highway district, support the TIF. The agency uses the revenues to repay the bonds issued to finance such public projects as land acquisition and demolition, construction of parking garages, and streetscaping. This was an important piece of legislation, signaling a loosening of the state's reins.

After the massive infusion of urban renewal program monies in the

1960s, federal development dollars have not flowed into Boise the way they have into some cities. For example, the city was not able to create a "pocket of poverty" to win a UDAG. (Boise has used some of its CDBG funds for parks and parking garages.) When the city received funding through an Economic Development Administration loan program in the mid-1980s, it tried to generate some activity in its moribund downtown area. The city put the funds into a zero-interest certificate of deposit so that local banks could use them to encourage private development through loans at lower than prime rates. Several downtown structures were rehabilitated through these loans, but this activity was too sporadic to stimulate additional development.

The prevailing philosophy in Boise may not support the extensive mobilization of public capital. One of the city's favorite homegrown industries, Micron Technologies, requested a waiver of its $1-million sewer hookup fee for its planned $90-million expansion. The city refused but negotiated a split fee, with the city paying 80 percent, Micron 20 percent. The city's argument is simple: if Micron were granted a waiver, the city would be hard pressed to withhold waivers from other firms, and the cumulative effect would be a drain on the city's treasury. Preferable to the city are negotiated agreements that allow the city to gauge costs and benefits on a project-by-project basis.

DULUTH

Duluth, mired in economic and social malaise since the mid-1970s shutdown of U.S. Steel and the many plant closings since then, became aggressive in promoting the city as a business location only since the early 1980s. Unemployment was well above the national average, emigration from the city left it with nearly 16 percent fewer inhabitants in a decade's time (1970–82), and general fund revenues declined in constant dollars. But the fragile fiscal foundation of the city did not mean city leaders were willing to risk tax revenues for high-risk development projects.

If Duluth's development efforts are characterized by one political constraint, it is that city development should never put general city tax receipts at risk. Instead, its development financial tools usually include a combination of one or more of the following: (1) tax-increment financing (TIF), (2) city-issued industrial revenue bonds, (3) federal and state funds, and (4) fee-based financing.

There are six TIF districts in Duluth. The entire downtown area is the largest; others include a mall, an industrial park, a truck center, a commercial area in the city's west end, and a waterfront development district. The creation of TIF districts requires the city to declare the area blighted. The county auditor's office establishes a value for the land and structures within the TIF district, and the city, school district, and county continue to receive property taxes equivalent to that base value for up to 25 years. Any increment in property values above the base is used by the city for acquisition and site preparation, debt repayment when TIF-backed bonds are issued (usually for infrastructure purposes), public improvements (such as financing the waterfront development), or any other purpose deemed important to redevelop the district. The two other overlapping authorities (the school district and county) then must forgo future property tax revenues from increases in property values until the statutory life of the TIF district expires (usually 25 years). For this reason, the city is required by the state to certify that the redevelopment projects would not have occurred without the assistance of the city's creation of a TIF district.

Industrial revenue bonds result in little risk for the city: the city does not pledge its full faith and credit, nor is there a moral obligation to repay debt holders in the event of default. Duluth, like all issuers of industrial bonds, must declare a public purpose for the bond, but unlike general obligation bonds, no pledge of general fund revenues is needed to support the project nor does a debt fund need to be established.

Federal and state funds are pursued vigorously by Duluth officials. It has received state financing in the form of enterprise zone credits, state funding for a convention center (requiring virtually no city investment), job-training grants, and other forms of state aid for the city's development efforts. Federal CDBG and UDAG funds also figure among the public finance incentives the city uses.

As a consequence of this deliberate strategy, general fund subsidies in the form of cash grants or forgone revenues, such as property tax abatement, are rarely considered. Even infrastructure provision, an element in nearly all cities' development bundles, is rarely provided except for fee-supported infrastructure, which requires the consumer to finance such infrastructure as sewer, water, gas, and steam. These infrastructures essentially are paid for by customers through charges on consumption and do not jeopardize or postpone general infrastructure projects, nor do they put a claim on future projects.

EVANSVILLE

Evansville offers fairly standard public financial incentives to developers; they tend to vary only marginally, depending principally on the location of the project. Typical incentives include tax abatement, federal and state funds for infrastructure, and if necessary issuance of general obligation bonds for infrastructure and redevelopment. Firms that locate in the city's vast enterprise zone are given an array of incentives, ranging from state income tax credits to a county tax credit on inventory.

The city's financial incentive plan invariably includes property tax abatement; as one development officer said, "I don't recall us ever turning down a tax abatement request." In the first year, the program abates 100 percent of all property taxes owed to the city, township, county, and school district, even though the property tax abatement decision is left strictly to the city government. In the second year, only 95 percent are abated; 80 percent are abated in the third year, 65 percent in the fourth, 50 percent in the fifth, 40 percent in the sixth, 30 percent in the seventh, 20 percent in the eighth, 10 percent in the ninth, and 5 percent in the tenth. As partial payment is made, those revenues are divided among the local governments according to their proportions of the total property tax rate. Since local governments in Indiana also levy a property tax on equipment, the city can also abate taxes on equipment for five years, according to a sliding scale.

The state has created an infrastructure program that provides federal grant funds to local governments on a competitive basis. The state also allows cities to designate blighted areas as enterprise zones. Firms locating in these zones are granted state tax credits and local inventory tax credits. Evansville has designated a large area encompassing parts of the central business district and older industrial sections of the city as its enterprise zone.

What is particularly interesting and most unusual about Evansville's development incentives, in the context of today's preponderance of fee-based public finance, is the conservative use of user fees or of any financing tool that places the costs of development directly on the beneficiary. Its fiscal and political philosophy seems to argue for financing through general taxation rather than through fees and charges. As a consequence, revenue bonds are almost unheard of (save for city utilities), tax increment bonds are permitted by the state but are not yet used by the city, user fees are kept to a minimum, and development and impact fees are nonexistent.

There appears to be a consensus that the risks and benefits associated with the city's public investments be spread across as many city residents and taxpayers as possible. Evansville is not situated in a wealthy part of the country, and its historic economic and demographic growth rates are modest. Consequently, officials are skeptical about building economic development on the hopes of a strong and rapidly growing economy. The future economic situation of Evansville, they seem to argue, will not be significantly better than it is today. Therefore, general taxes and forgone general tax revenues in the form of property tax abatement are heavily relied on for development incentives.

HUNTSVILLE

The development tools used in Huntsville are both extensive and ephemeral; the city goes to great lengths to support a project it deems worthy, but its hand is seldom discerned. And that is just the way the city wants it. One of its main development tools is of an organizational nature: the city has created myriad development authorities. Besides providing organizational and financial flexibility, below market-rate financing, and property tax abatement, these authorities serve two useful purposes: first, the debt accumulated by an authority does not affect the state-imposed debt-equity ratio for cities; second, an authority provides a buffer between city leaders and development decisions.

All three of the significant development projects undertaken in Huntsville from the mid-1960s through the 1980s involve authorities. Cummings Research Park, a 3,600-acre high-technology park that was established and nutured by the city, is legally a creature of Huntsville's Industrial Development Board. The Chrysler/Acu-star facility and the related international intermodal transporation system at the airport, again actively supported by the city, are managed by the joint city-county Airport Authority. And the showplace of downtown Huntsville, the Von Braun Civic Center complex, is operated by a separate convention center authority. Huntsville's use of development authorities continues to be a key development tool. In anticipation of a future downtown renewal project along the lines of San Antonio's river walk, there is now talk of the creation of a downtown redevelopment authority.

Huntsville has other tools at its disposal. It uses annexation, utility provision, and infrastructure installation as mechanisms to promote development. Frequently, these three tools (along with some land banking) are used in concert. In the 1960s, Huntsville doubled its territory, extended utility coverage to the annexed areas (Huntsville operates the largest municipal utilities operation in Alabama), and installed the infrastructure. Since then, the city has "encouraged" adjacent areas to become part of Huntsville by refusing to extend city sewer facilities outside its boundaries. Recently, Huntsville took its utilities "across the mountain" to an area traditionally considered beyond the city's sphere of influence. By incorporating the area into the city, and also by annexing 12,000 acres in Limestone County on the western side of the city, Huntsville has ensured two growth corridors of almost unlimited potential.

Typically, investment in transportation infrastructure is considered a nonspecific development tool financed largely by nonlocal governments. In Huntsville, however, transportation is a key component of the city's development strategy. The city was left out of the interstate highway system. (At the time, Decatur was the larger city, and highway planners expected it to emerge as the dominant city in northern Alabama.) For a city with visions as grand as Huntsville's, the inaccessibility of an interstate highway has negatively affected its development. In an effort to minimize the damage, the city has agreed to assume the state's portion of the costs of an interstate spur (I-565) and related roadway improvements. The project costs are estimated to be in the $74-million range. In this specific instance, the city (as well as the county) are absorbing real financial costs at the rate of approximately 30 cents on the dollar. In their calculus, if local governments did not pay the state's matching share, the roadwork would be unacceptably delayed.

INDEPENDENCE

In Independence the supply of development tools is limited, their use modest. Some of the city's conservatism is a function of the larger Missouri context. In a state that requires a referendum on any kind of local tax increase, one would not expect a city to offer revenue-draining incentives to promote development. Another explanation for the city's reluctance to mobilize public capital rests in the lack of consensus among local officials and opinion leaders as to Independence's future.

The city engages in land assemblage and infrastructure installation as a means of guiding development. A review of recent projects provides no consistent development support pattern but rather case-by-case assistance. For example, the city sold surplus land "at a reasonable rate" to a local nonprofit development corporation for the creation of an industrial park. The city provided the labor and equipment for infrastructure installation (streets, sewers, and utilities), the nonprofit organization paid for the materials. Profits from the sales of the improved parcels provided the revenues for the nonprofit organization to undertake an expansion of the park without city assistance. In another case, the city helped pay for the construction of a storm water detention facility for a major shopping center project. (The developers and a state grant paid for the rest.) In addition, an ordinance allows the city to reduce utility rates to enhance development. However, given that utility service charges generate two-thirds of the city's revenues, Independence has been reluctant to offer this incentive. In one departure, however, the city offered free utility service for up to five years to a developer attempting to site a museum to display artifacts from a steamship that had sunk in the Missouri River in 1860. (The developer declined the offer in favor of a "better deal" from another community.)

Independence uses its CDBG funds for economic development. (According to one estimate, in the late 1980s, as much as 74 percent of the city's CDBG funds were going for capital improvements.) Independence has used these funds to finance the rehabilitation of two historic properties. One property was deeded to the city; the other was purchased with the assistance of private donations.

Over time, the state has provided the legal authority for local governments to try some newer development tools. For example, Missouri Act 353 enables the creation of local redevelopment corporations with the power to grant tax abatements. Independence has established a redevelopment corporation for Independence Square, the traditional downtown area. Its primary redevelopment activity has been improvement of building facades. Missouri has adopted an enterprise zone statute, but Independence has not been able to assemble census tracts in a manner that qualifies for enterprise zone designation. In addition, Missouri has enacted a tax-increment financing provision. There was some discussion of using tax-increment financing in the redevelopment of South Square, a decaying area near downtown Independence. However, the city eventually decided to use CDBG funds for the project.

LOWELL

Lowell counts among the elements of its public finance package for development the following: state funds, city-issued industrial revenue bonds, general obligation bonds, eminent domain takings, UDAG and CDBG funds, and the active involvement of two pivotal, nonprofit organizations, the Lowell Plan, Inc., and the Lowell Development and Financial Corporation (LDFC). Lowell's basic philosophy for selecting development tools relies on a well-established and successful formula: entertain a number of public financial packages but always, always include the Lowell Plan.

In addition to a receptive City Hall and city participation in the Lowell Plan and the LDFC, Lowell has enjoyed unusual success in securing federal aid in the form of grants, loans, and programs. In 1978 the creation of the Lowell National Historical Park in the heart of the city by the federal government guaranteed long-term financial support for Lowell not only for its tourism-generating capabilities but also for its historic preservation grants and loans. The Historic Preservation Commission makes low-interest loans to businesses in the historic preservation district (which encompasses nearly all of Lowell's central business district) to renovate the facades of the buildings. This program is administered by the LDFC, another sign of the intricate ties among development organizations. Furthermore, the commission is a member of the Lowell Plan.

Like most American cities, Lowell seeks federal and state assistance whenever possible. UDAG funds are applied for routinely, and the city has been quite successful in securing them since its initial grant in 1978 for the relocation of Wang Industries. In fact, Lowell received six UDAGs totaling more than $14 million. CDBG funds are also used for development purposes.

The high population density of the urban areas of Massachusetts has made parking spaces a premium. Indeed, the area within the political boundaries of Lowell is only 13.38 square miles, or approximately 6,500 persons per square mile. The state created an off-street parking program to help local governments build adequate parking facilities for commuters; all four of Lowell's parking garages built since the mid-1970s have been partially financed by these state funds.

High on the list of development tools is the city's authority to take private property for public purposes—or eminent domain. Although used liberally in the past, this is bound to change. In 1988 alone the city's eminent domain action was challenged six times. It lost two cases in court, one was settled out of court, and three were still in court. All six owners challenged the size of the city's monetary offering for their property. Lowell will probably settle these financial claims by drawing down accumulated end-of-year general fund surpluses. Eminent domain takings are now considered highly risky because of the long-term costs to the city. The political costs are also extraordinary.

Lowell is responsible for the public school system, which for the past several years has clamored for increased funding (primarily as a consequence of the unexpected influx of migrants from Southeast Asia). The general fund surplus could have provided at least partial support for the school system's needs; now, it appears that most of it will go to those who had their property taken for public purposes. The cost to the city for these six challenges could exceed $4 million—a considerable sum for a city that doesn't invest cash in development projects.

Although cash contributions for development projects are not considered part of the city's investment pool, Lowell does issue general obligation bonds for development projects, which represent the city's full faith and credit, and as such forms part of the city's investment bundle.

ORLANDO

Orlando, unlike most of the cities in our study, does not have a typical or standard incentive offering to developers. Each project, therefore, is somewhat different from the others. Nevertheless, two important tools are relied on, and these two tools are frequently employed together. First, the city created a Downtown Development Board charged with regenerating Orlando's central business district. Within this district, however, a smaller area of 569 acres was carved out as a tax increment financing district and placed under the purview of the Community Redevelopment Agency. Second, the city purchases land through the Development Board and uses it as part of a leveraging strategy in promoting development. Most often, land is used as the city's form of participation in joint ventures with the private sector.

Because of the booming economy and high demand for real estate in the Orlando metropolitan area, the city expects to generate a handsome return from its development projects. For example, the Church Street project (retail shops, restaurants, and a parking garage adjacent to a

Rouse festival marketplace project) expected to generate an 11 percent return on its investment (i.e., the value of the land) in addition to lease payments from the developer who built the project. In fact, because of the high demand for Orlando's real estate, all city investments in economic development projects are expected to generate a profit to the city or to the Development Board. An entrepreneurial spirit certainly captures the attitude of Orlando's city officials.

An example of this entrepreneurial behavior (and resulting "profits" to the city) is a highly visible City Hall project. A developer was given a 75-year lease on 6.7 acres of city-owned land on which the old City Hall stood. The developer agreed to construct and finance three buildings: two private buildings of 400,000 to 500,000 square feet and one public building (the new City Hall) of 200,000 square feet. The costs of these buildings were to be borne by the developer. The new City Hall effectively was built, then, with private dollars. Moreover, the cost of imploding the old City Hall was paid for by a film company that filmed the building's destruction and used the scene in its movie, *Lethal Weapon 3*.

SANTA BARBARA

Santa Barbara does not offer money or underwrite programs for commercial rehabilitations. It provides no low-interest subsidies for business. It offers no tax abatement. It sponsors no economic development promotion. It conducts no industrial recruitment. There is no program in Santa Barbara to leverage private investment, nor is there a public-private partnership. This city has neither a tax-services imbalance nor the aspirations that trigger development promotion in other cities. Instead Santa Barbara's regulatory power represents a vast store of public capital, and the city is not hesitant to mobilize it.

City assistance or involvement in development often is nothing more than approval of a proposed project. The dominant policy instrument is the city's comprehensive plan. The intent is to ensure that development is acceptable—that it fits the plan. Zoning variances, manipulation of the parking supply, and the imposition of fees are additional tools. The city does not promote development the way other cities do; instead, Santa Barbara attempts to mold it.

The city does make improvements to commons land that benefits adjacent businesses. For example, the city might install decorative landscaping along a street. But these tools—plaza improvements, parking lot development—provide only limited assistance to developers. The market is strong; no exodus of business from the redevelopment area has occurred, and development is bolstered by an active local financial market. Few out-of-town, big-money developers populate the Santa Barbara market. Instead, local property owners are the developers, and local banks provide the capital.

The TIF district that was created in downtown Santa Barbara in 1975 provides revenues and fiscal flexibility for the city. Bond sales financed the revitalization of three blocks of State Street (Santa Barbara's "Main Street") and the Paseo Nuevo Retail Center project. Assessed value in the Central City Redevelopment Project area continues to rise, thereby increasing the increment. The city's revenues from the incremental value increased 98.8 percent in five years.

Santa Barbara does not hesitate to acquire, improve, and resell land. When selling property, government agencies must offer it first to other government entities, and the city recently bought land from the school board, paying $1.5 million in cash. The city used half the land for a parking lot for downtown workers and sold the other half for its appraised value ($0.5 million), placing stipulations on its development.

In 1989 the city condemned land to construct a parking garage in anticipation of the demand related to a large new downtown retail project (Paseo Nuevo). The city also built a separate structure on the site, which it intended to sell as commercial property. Under state law, if condemnation proceedings are used to acquire the property, the prior owner is offered participation in the redeveloped parcel. Had the previous owner not wanted to exercise this option, then the agency would retain the structure and lease it out. The value of the retail space jumped from $600,000 to $1.2 million from the time of condemnation to the completion of the parking garage. The city plans to construct paseos between the parking facility and adjacent businesses, using condemnation to take the land. There were parking spaces behind some of the buildings next to the planned paseos, but in the view of the city that parking would detract from the attractiveness of the paseos. The city opened the garage on a Monday. On Tuesday the city notified the property owners of the intended condemnation and erected barriers to their existing parking. This is development, Santa Barbara style.

SPRINGFIELD

As a consequence of the general aversion toward city-led investment, Springfield is left with two local investment tools, neither of which costs the city any direct transfer of funds and one of which will become less important in the near future. The first is tax abatement; the city might offer tax abatement to prospective developers who locate in—or expand within—the city's vast enterprise zone. Although enterprise zone legislation was approved by the state in 1985, it was not until 1987 that Springfield established its own enterprise zone. Prior to 1987, tax abatement could be offered to firms within the community reinvestment zone.

Property taxes are abated for 30 years at 100 percent; but the forgone tax revenues from granting tax abatement do not affect city financing, because the city is dependent upon the income tax and does not (effectively) levy a property tax. County and school districts bear the brunt of this development tool, yet they have no legal voice in the decision. Because of the controversy surrounding city-granted tax abatement that has no effect on city finances, Springfield recently proposed to include the school district in the decisionmaking process.

Tax abatement has been granted to only five firms since 1980. Its infrequent use, however, appears to be more a function of a weak local economy than a conscious effort to hide the incentive or to make it difficult to obtain. If requested, city officials seem more than willing to offer it to prospective firms and developers. Furthermore, firms requesting tax abatement must certify that half of all new employees are residents of the city.

The second public finance tool is the acquisition and sale of real estate for development. This activity is restricted to the city's central business district and was initially financed in the mid-1970s with a 0.5 percent increase in the city income tax. The income tax increase was used in part to build City Hall and to bring commercial establishments and offices back to the central business district by acquiring, renovating, and razing blighted buildings. Credit Life Insurance Company (CLICO) leased land adjacent to City Hall for 30 years and, because the land is tax-exempt, pays an annual in-lieu-of tax of approximately $96,000 to the city's tax-equivalency fund (a tax-increment fund), which in turn is a dedicated city fund for renovating and refurbishing downtown Springfield.

This tool, however, is not available to areas other than the central business district. This financing tool is highly unusual in that the in-lieu-of tax is equivalent to the property owner's total property tax bill (that is, combined school, county, township, and city property taxes). And the city does not share the fund with the other local governments. That is to say, the city required CLICO to contribute an equivalent amount of property taxes to the tax-equivalency fund even though, had the property not been tax-exempt, the property tax revenues would have been divided among all levels of local government. The city, because of its almost nonexistent property tax rate, would have received next to nothing.

City-owned real estate is a limited development finance tool, because this land is leased or granted to developers. In 1989, after agreeing to provide land for a civic center, the city had very little land left from its core redevelopment. Furthermore, even this land incentive had political costs, because some taxpayers did not separate cash grants (from the general fund) from land grants. As the mayor pointed out, "Even the land grant to the hotel and civic center projects generated taxpayer hostility because those were perceived as tax dollars."

Springfield, a city with few financial offerings for developers, has turned to the state capital and to Washington for supplemental funds. The state has been instrumental in ensuring a flow of incentives. In 1982, for example, International Harvester, an important Springfield employer, decided to consolidate its plant operations in either Springfield or Ft. Wayne, Indiana. The millions of dollars in incentives (job retraining, tax abatement, etc.) were granted by the state. The city was aggressive in securing International Harvester's agreement to remain in Springfield, but the financial tools to induce the company to stay in Springfield were primarily from the state. Seven years after the company decided on the Springfield site, employment by the company (renamed Navistar) declined substantially. Navistar has two sites, one in the city (the original building) and the other (a newer, more expensive facility) outside the city. Only approximately one-third of the employees live in the city, meaning income taxes from two-thirds of the employees are paid elsewhere. Property taxes associated with both facilities benefit not the city (because of the nearly nonexistent property tax) but other local governments.

NOTES

PREFACE AND ACKNOWLEDGMENTS

1. Dennis R. Judd, "From Cowtown to Sunbelt City: Boosterism and Economic Growth in Denver," in Susan S. Fainstein et al., eds. *Restructuring the City* (New York: Longman, 1983), p. 172.

2. R. D. Norton, *City Life Cycles and American Urban Policy* (New York: Academic, 1979); Ross J. Gittell, *Renewing Cities* (Princeton: Princeton University Press, 1992).

3. Alf Nucifora, as quoted in Charles Mahtesian, "The Selling of the States," *Governing* 7 (Jan. 1994): 44–47, 47.

CHAPTER I / POLITICS MATTERS

1. See Carter Goodrich, *Government Promotion of American Canals and Railroads, 1800–1890* (New York: Columbia University Press, 1960); Louis Hartz, *Economic Policy and Democratic Thought: Pennsylvania, 1776–1868* (Cambridge: Harvard University Press, 1948); Alfred J. Watkins, *The Practice of Urban Economics* (Beverly Hills, Calif.: Sage, 1980).

2. "Railroad entrepreneurs quickly became adept at playing cities off against one another to get the most lucrative subsidies." Dennis R. Judd and Todd Swanstrom, *City Politics: Private Power and Public Policy* (New York: Harper-Collins, 1994), p. 26.

3. Paul E. Peterson, *City Limits* (Chicago: University of Chicago Press, 1981).

4. Clarence N. Stone, *Regime Politics: Governing Atlanta, 1946–1988* (Lawrence: University Press of Kansas, 1989).

5. Ann O'M. Bowman, *Tools and Targets: The Mechanics of City Economic Development* (Washington, D.C.: National League of Cities, 1987).

6. General Accounting Office, *Urban Development Action Grants: Effects of the 1987 Amendments on Project Selection* (Washington, D.C.: GAO, 1989).

7. For Francis Lowell's thoughts on Lowell as the textile center of the world, see Thomas Bender, *Toward an Urban Vision: Ideas and Institutions in Nineteenth-Century America* (1975; Baltimore: Johns Hopkins Press, 1982).

8. Former U.S. Senator Paul Tsongas was less charitable in his characterization of Lowell, claiming that "No . . . city was in worse shape than Lowell by 1970." *Horizon*, June 1985, p. 33.

9. For a discussion of the impact of the war years on Lowell's economy, see Marc S. Miller, *The Irony of Victory: World War II and Lowell, Massachusetts* (Urbana: University of Illinois Press, 1988).

10. "Coming Soon: Hollywood, the Sequel," *Newsweek,* Feb. 6, 1989.

11. "Orlando's Magic Kingdom," *Newsweek,* Sept. 2, 1985, p. 43.

12. Stephen Kindel, "Dueling with the Mouse King," *Financial World,* May 19, 1987, p. 42; Robert Guskind, "The Mouse that Roared," *National Journal,* Apr. 30, 1994, 1009–14.

13. For a still relevant, yet dated, study of the politics, economics, and geography of Duluth, see Daniel Elazar, "Constitutional Change in a Long-Depressed Community: A Case Study of Duluth, Minnesota," *Journal of the Minnesota Academy of Science* 33, no. 1 (1965): 49–66.

14. The dreams and failures of the city were the highlight of the entire 58th Special Anniversary Issue of *Newsweek* (Spring 1983).

15. City of Springfield, *Comprehensive Annual Financial Report for Fiscal Year Ended December 31, 1987.*

16. L. J. Davis, "Unlikely, but Boise Means Big Business," *New York Times Magazine,* June 11, 1989, p. 24.

17. These figures were derived from *Independence Employment Overview* (Independence, Mo.: Mid-America Regional Council, 1988).

CHAPTER 2 / PUBLIC CAPITAL, SYSTEMS OF
CITIES, AND PERCEPTUAL ORBITS

1. John R. Logan and Harvey L. Molotch, *Urban Fortunes* (Berkeley: University of California Press, 1987).

2. Ideas expressed by Peterson, *City Limits;* Bernard J. Frieden and Lynne B. Sagalyn, *Downtown, Inc.: How America Rebuilds Cities* (Cambridge: MIT Press, 1989); Ted Robert Gurr and Desmond S. King, *The State and the City* (Chicago: University of Chicago Press, 1987); and Stone, *Regime Politics,* respectively.

3. Subjectivity and its importance in decisionmakers' choices are systematically addressed in Stephen H. Linder and B. Guy Peters, "Instruments of Government: Perceptions and Contexts," *Journal of Public Policy* 9 (1989): 35–58.

4. See, for example, the discussion in John Petersen and Catherine Spain, *Essays in Public Finance/Public Management* (Chatham, N.J.: Chatham House, 1979); Emil Malizia, *Local Economic Development: A Guide to Practice* (New York: Praeger, 1985); and Edward J. Blakely, *Planning Local Economic Development: Theory and Practice* (Newbury Park, Calif.: Sage, 1989).

5. Harold Wolman, "Local Economic Development Policy: What Explains the Divergence Between Policy Analysis and Political Behavior," *Journal of Urban Affairs* 10 (1988): 19–28, 27.

6. See, for example, the discussion in Kenneth K. Wong, "Economic Constraint and Political Choice in Urban Policymaking," *American Journal of Political Science* 32 (1988): 1–18; and Robert J. Waste, *The Ecology of City Policymaking* (New York: Oxford University Press, 1989).

Development decisions have been studied in Gittell, *Renewing Cities;* and Bryan D. Jones and Lynn W. Bachelor, *The Sustaining Hand,* 2d ed. (Lawrence: University Press of Kansas, 1993).

7. The conceptual framework first appeared in Ann O'M. Bowman and Michael A. Pagano, "City Intervention: An Analysis of the Public Capital Mobilization Process," *Urban Affairs Quarterly* 27 (Mar. 1992): 356–74. Reaction to it has led to the refined argument presented here.

8. Peter Eisinger categorizes the economic development policy instruments available to governments as either supply-side or demand-side. Supply-side policies attempt to stimulate investment by lowering the costs associated with production. Demand-side policies are more market sensitive and thrust governments into a more entrepreneurial mode. Contemporary economic development policy is increasingly demand-side. See Peter K. Eisinger, *The Rise of the Entrepreneurial State* (Madison: University of Wisconsin Press, 1988).

9. Linder and Peters, "Instruments of Government."

10. Margery Ambrosius, for example, raises questions about the political benefits derived from economic development policy. See Margery M. Ambrosius, "Are Political Benefits the Only Benefits of State Economic Development Policies?" paper prepared for the Annual Meeting of the American Political Science Association, San Francisco, 1990. Certainly, political benefits are generated from rebalancing the tax-services relation or from taking the city to a new economic plane. In one of our study cities, a new mayor was widely credited with creating a vision that moved the city beyond its long-standing subregional status into a more regional position. The mayor was subsequently successful in his bid for a statewide office (for U.S. Senate).

11. In its pure form, city hierarchy analysis imposes a rigid uniformity on a system of cities. As a consequence, such analysis has been subjected to numerous modifications and extensions, such as Thierry J. Noyelle and Thomas N. Stanback's classification of metropolitan areas into nodal centers, specialized service centers, production centers, and consumer-oriented centers. See their volume, *The Economic Transformation of American Cities* (Totowa, N.J.: Rowman and Allanheld, 1983). Within each of the types of centers are subgroups that reflect population size and economic function. City hierarchy analysis cannot differentiate great cities from cities that are simply large. See Emrys Jones, *Metropolis* (Oxford: Oxford University Press, 1990), especially chap. 1, for a discussion of this point.

12. Ann O'M. Bowman, "Competition for Economic Development Among Southeastern Cities," *Urban Affairs Quarterly* 23 (June 1988): 511–27.

13. For a discussion of the role of leadership in economic development, see Dennis Judd and Michael Parkinson, eds., *Leadership and Urban Regeneration* (Newbury Park, Calif.: Sage, 1990); and Lynn W. Bachelor, "Leadership and Economic Development Policy in Eight Midwestern Cities," paper prepared for the Annual Meeting of the Southern Political Science Association, Tampa, 1991.

14. Harold Wolman argues that "the mental maps of local political elites are related to elite behavior." See Harold Wolman, "Local Government and the Citizen: Citizen Participation and the Mental Maps of Political Elites," paper prepared for the European Consortium for Political Research, Limerick, Ireland, 1992, p. 12.

15. The term *urban village* has been employed in Phoenix and is acclaimed by Christopher B. Leinberger and Charles Lockwood, "How Business Is Reshaping America," *Atlantic Monthly,* Oct. 1986, 43–52.

16. Philip Langdon, "A Good Place to Live," *Atlantic Monthly*, Mar. 1988, p. 56.

17. Joel Garreau, *Edge City: Life on the New Frontier* (New York: Doubleday, 1991).

18. Mark Schneider, *The Competitive City: The Political Economy of Suburbia* (Pittsburgh: University of Pittsburgh Press, 1989), p. 164.

19. Todd Swanstrom, *The Crisis of Growth Politics* (Philadelphia: Temple University Press, 1986).

20. Richard Cyert and James March, *A Behavioral Theory of the Firm* (Englewood Cliffs, N.J.: Prentice-Hall, 1963).

21. Charles Tiebout, "A Pure Theory of Public Expenditures," *Journal of Political Economy* 44 (1956): 416–24.

22. Paul E. Peterson, Barry Rabe, and Kenneth K. Wong, *When Federalism Works* (Washington, D.C.: Brookings, 1986), p. 13.

23. Cyert and March, *A Behavioral Theory of the Firm.*

24. See, for example, the discussion in Harold Wolman, "Understanding Local Government Response to Fiscal Pressure," *Journal of Public Policy* 3 (1983): 245–64; and Michael A. Pagano, "Fiscal Disruptions and City Responses: Stability, Equilibrium, and City Capital Spending," *Urban Affairs Quarterly* 23 (1988): 118–37.

25. Helen Ladd and John Yinger, *America's Ailing Cities: Fiscal Health and the Design of Urban Policy* (Baltimore: Johns Hopkins Press, 1989).

26. Elaine Sharp finds that "fiscal trouble triggers the adoption of development policies." See her "Institutional Manifestations of Accessibility and Urban Economic Development Policy," *Western Political Quarterly* 44 (Mar. 1991): 129–47; 138.

27. Gainesville, a university community in north-central Florida, is a case in point. As Ronald Vogel and Bert Swanson note, the city's support of development has varied with the electoral fortunes of the progrowth and managed growth factions on the city commission. See Ronald K. Vogel and Bert E. Swanson, "The Growth Machine versus the Antigrowth Coalition," *Urban Affairs Quarterly* 25 (Sept. 1989): 63–85.

28. Albert Schaffer, "The Houston Growth Coalition in 'Boom' and 'Bust,'" *Journal of Urban Affairs* 11 (1989): 21–38.

29. Harry Richardson, *Regional Economics* (New York: Praeger, 1969), p. 156.

30. M. Jarvin Emerson and F. Charles Lamphear, *Urban and Regional Economics* (Boston: Allyn and Bacon, 1975), p. 96.

31. Gordon Mulligan, "Tinberger-type Central Place Systems," *International Regional Science Review,* 7, no. 1 (1982): 83–91, 83.

32. Conceptual clarifications and empirical studies based on central-place theory abound in academic literature. For a recent example, see Xiao-Ping Zheng, "The Spatial Structure of Hierarchical Interurban Systems," *Journal of Regional Science* 30, no. 3 (1990): 375–92.

33. Richardson, *Regional Economics,* p. 160; see also Emerson and Lamphear, *Urban and Regional Economics,* p. 97.

34. Keith S. O. Beavon, *Central Place Theory: A Reinterpretation* (London: Longman, 1977), p. 6.

35. Attribution of the intellectual origins of central-place theory to von Thünen is noted in Harvey S. Perloff and Lowdon Wingo Jr., introduction to Perloff and Wingo, eds., *Issues in Urban Economics* (Baltimore: Johns Hopkins Press, 1968), p. 5.

36. See Brian Berry, *Geography of Market Centers and Retail Distribution* (Englewood Cliffs, N.J.: Prentice-Hall, 1967), p. 13.

37. Katherine L. Bradbury, Anthony Downs, and Kenneth A. Small, *Urban Decline and the Future of American Cities* (Washington, D.C.: Brookings, 1982).

38. Norman J. Glickman and Robert H. Wilson, "National Contexts for Urban Economic Policy," in Edward M. Bergman, ed., *Local Economies in Transition* (Durham: Duke University Press, 1986); and Carl Abbott, *The Metropolitan Frontier: Cities in the Modern American West* (Tucson: University of Arizona Press, 1993).

39. Margit Mayer, "Local Politics: From Administration to Management," paper prepared for the Cardiff Symposium on Regulation, Innovation, and Spatial Development, University of Wales, 1989.

40. John D. Kasarda, "The Implications of Contemporary Redistribution Trends for National Urban Policy," *Social Science Quarterly* 61 (Dec. 1980): 373–400.

41. Brian J. L. Berry, *Growth Centers in the American Urban System,* vol. 1 (Cambridge: Ballinger, 1973).

42. See *Rand McNally Map of Trading Areas* (Chicago).

43. Local officials' visions of their city's place in the relevant hierarchy are, of course, influenced by actors in the private sector. Indeed, their vision is frequently influenced by a business elite, not unlike the Atlanta group, with a strong interest in personal profit. By encouraging their city to move to a higher plane, these private individuals stand to gain monetarily. For an account of the influence of the business elite on city governance and public policy, see Stone, *Regime Politics.*

44. Richardson, *Regional Economics,* pp. 162–63.

45. Noyelle and Stanback, *Economic Transformation of American Cities.*

46. President's Commission for a National Agenda for the Eighties, *Urban America in the 1980s* (Washington, D.C.: Government Printing Office, 1980); Department of Housing and Urban Development, *National Urban Policy Report* (Washington, D.C.: Government Printing Office, 1982).

47. Advisory Commission on Intergovernmental Relations, *Federal Preemption of State and Local Authority* (Washington, D.C.: ACIR, 1989); General Accounting Office, *Federal-State-Local Relations: Trends of the Past Decade and Emerging Issues* (Washington, D.C.: GAO, 1990).

48. Michael A. Pagano, "Cities' Responses to Tax Reform," *Municipal Finance Journal* 10, no. 4 (1989): 319–33; Dennis Zimmerman, *The Private Use of Tax-Exempt Bonds: Controlling Public Subsidy of Private Activity* (Washington, D.C.: Urban Institute, 1990).

49. The cases can be found, respectively, in 469 U.S. 528 (1985); and 108 S.Ct. 1355 (1988).

50. Anthony Orum, for example, cites the protracted battles between the city of Milwaukee and the state of Wisconsin over matters of territorial domination. See Anthony Orum, "Apprehending the City: The View from Above, Below, and Behind," *Urban Affairs Quarterly* 26 (June 1991): 589–609.

251. See Jon Teaford, "City vs. State: The Struggle for Legal Ascendancy," *American Journal of Legal History* 17, no. 1 (1973): 51–65.

52. *Clinton v. Cedar Rapids and Missouri River Railroad,* 24 Iowa 455 (1868).

53. Advisory Commission on Intergovernmental Relations, "State Laws Governing Local Government and Administration," draft version. Washington, D.C., Sept. 1992.

54. The state of Washington created the Public Works Trust Fund to help provide local infrastructure. Ohio issued $120 million annually for 10 years to improve local infrastructure and enhance local development. Massachusetts, Vermont, Illinois, and other states developed infrastructure bond banks. See, e.g., C. Kurt Zorn and Shaw Towfighi, "Not All Bond Banks Are Created Equal," *Public Budgeting & Finance* 6, no. 3 (1986): 57–69.

CHAPTER 3 / ASPIRATIONS, VISIONS, AND IMAGES

1. Lewis Mumford, "What Is a City?" in Donald L. Miller, ed., *The Lewis Mumford Reader* (New York: Pantheon, 1986), p. 104.

2. Donald L. Miller, "The Urban Prospect: Introduction," in ibid., p. 157.

3. Kenneth Boulding, *The Image* (Ann Arbor: University of Michigan Press, 1956).

4. See two articles: George Sternlieb, "The City as Sandbox," and Norton Long, "The City as Reservation," both in *Public Interest* 25, no. 1 (1971): 14–21 and 22–38, respectively.

5. Peter Langer, "Sociology—Four Images of Organized Diversity: Bazaar, Jungle, Organism, and Machine," in Lloyd Rodwin and Robert M. Hollister, eds., *Cities of the Mind* (New York: Plenum, 1984).

6. Rosellen Brown, "A City Whose Image Belies Its Vision," *Nation's Cities Weekly,* June 25, 1990, pp. 1, 8.

7. As quoted in Anselm L. Strauss, *Images of the American City* (New York: Free Press of Glencoe, 1961), p. 14.

8. Kevin Lynch, *The Image of the City* (Cambridge: MIT Press, 1960), pp. 2, 9.

9. Strauss, *Images of the American City,* p. 8.

10. Robert Lipsyte, "What Is Baseball Without Beer Ads?" *New York Times,* Oct. 25, 1991.

11. Detroit leaders have undertaken to change in their city's image, hoping for nothing short of what Boulding calls conversion. Detroit's campaign is designed 2to publicize the positive aspects of the city. Some observers, however, claim that Detroit's negative image is, in fact, an accurate reflection of a city plagued by a large budget deficit, inferior schools, deteriorated neighborhoods, and a high homicide rate. See Charles Child, "Detroit Unveils Image Campaign," *City & State,* Oct. 8, 1990, p. 45.

12. Strauss, *Images of the American City,* p. 13.

13. Sharon Zukin, *Landscapes of Power: From Detroit to Disney World* (Berkeley: University of California Press, 1991), p. 219.

14. Charles Paul Freund, "The L.A. Fantasy Goes the Way of All Flesh," *Washington Post National Weekly Edition,* May 11–17, 1992, p. 25.

15. Ibid.

16. Mayer, "Local Politics."

17. Ibid., p. 12.

18. Frances Frank Marcus, "New Orleans Entertains a Casino Plan," *New York Times,* May 1, 1992. Despite the imagery generated by opponents, potential jobs and tax revenues were powerful inducements. The Louisiana legislature approved enabling legislation for the casino in June 1992.

19. J. Harold Chandler, as quoted in Tom Walker, "Image-Building Drive Has Given Columbia Plenty to be Proud Of," *Atlanta Journal and Constitution,* Mar. 20, 1988.

20. Harvey Molotch, "The Political Economy of Growth Machines," paper prepared for the Annual Meeting of the American Political Science Association, Washington, D.C., Aug. 29–Sept. 1, 1991.

21. Howard Mansfield, *Cosmopolis: Yesterday's Cities of the Future* (New Brunswick, N.J.: Center for Urban Policy Research, Rutgers University, 1990), p. 32.

22. Quoted in Anne Raver, "An Odd Hybrid Called Ameriflora Struggles in Ohio," *New York Times,* Aug. 6, 1992.

23. Peterson, *City Limits.*

24. Jim Morrill and David Perlmutt, "World-Class City? Some Voters Say, So What?," *Charlotte Observer,* Sept. 1, 1991.

25. Although professional sports franchises validate a city's importance, the question of world-class status is a matter for debate. According to Jane Jacobs, "what makes a world-class city is subjective. . . . It's like beauty; it's in the eye of the beholder." As quoted in Chris Reidy, "Life Is Not Football," *Boston Globe,* Jan. 30, 1994.

26. See, for example, M. Gottdiener and Alexandros Ph. Lagopoulos, eds., *The City and the Sign: An Introduction to Urban Semiotics* (New York: Columbia University Press, 1986).

27. M. Gottdiener, "Culture, Ideology, and the Sign of the City," in Gottdiener and Lagopoulous, *The City and the Sign,* p. 206.

28. Raymond Ledrut, "The Images of the City," in Gottdiener and Lagopoulos, eds., *The City and the Sign,* p. 222.

29. Gottdiener, "Culture, Ideology, and the Sign of the City," pp. 209, 216.

30. Gerald D. Suttles, "The Cumulative Texture of Local Urban Culture," *American Journal of Sociology* 90 (Sept. 1984): 283–304, 284.

31. Wolman, "Local Government and the Citizen."

32. For examples, see Melinda Beck, "Lowell: A Town Is Reborn," *Newsweek,* Sept. 28, 1981, pp. 28–30; George Jones, "'High Tech' Ends a Long Slump in an Old Mill Town," *US News & World Report,* Apr. 6, 1981, pp. 64–65; Geraldine Brooks, "The Road Back: Old New England City Heals Itself: Can One in Midwest Do So Too?" *Wall Street Journal,* Feb. 1, 1985; Dorothy Schechter, "Lowell: Mill Town Renaissance," *Horizon,* June 1985, pp. 25–40.

33. Patricia M. Flynn, "Lowell: A High Tech Success Story," in David Lampe, ed., *The Massachusetts Miracle* (Cambridge: MIT Press, 1988), p. 285.

34. In fact, Tampa's daily newspaper, the *Tampa Tribune,* published a long article on Orlando that barely managed to conceal the Cigar City's envy of its cross-state rival. Tampa's mayor commented: "I don't want to live in Orlando. I don't want to live in a community that is a series of theme parks." See Wayne Garcia, "Orlando: A Downtown Booms," *Tampa Tribune,* May 3, 1992.

35. City of Independence, "Tourism Marketing Plan," April 1989, p. 33.

36. Rochelle Bookspan, ed., *Santa Barbara by the Sea* (Santa Barbara: McNally and Lofton, 1982), p. 53.

37. Beaumont has cautiously embraced the new tools, joining with Jefferson County to establish a state enterprise zone at the old Bethlehem Steel property, and the city is issuing tax-increment financing for the restoration of the Tyrrell Historical Library. The establishment of the TIF district was unsuccessfully opposed by the Beaumont Independent School District, which depends heavily on property tax revenues.

CHAPTER 4 / CITIES AND
ECONOMIC DEVELOPMENT

1. Michael J. Wolkoff, "Economic Development Financing Policy: A State and Local Perspective," in Richard D. Bingham, Edward W. Hill, and Sammis B. White, eds., *Financing Economic Development: An Institutional Response* (Newbury Park, Calif.: Sage, 1990), p. 30.

2. The literature on market failure blossomed during the 1980s. For a review and detailed discussion of market failures, see Charles Wolf Jr., "Market and Non-Market Failures: Comparison and Assessment," *Journal of Public Policy* 7, no. 1 (1987): 43–70; David L. Weimer and Aidan R. Vining, *Policy Analysis: Concepts and Practice,* 2d ed. (Englewood Cliffs, N.J.: Prentice-Hall, 1989), pp. 30–93. The market failures listed herein are derived from Weimer and Vining, *Policy Analysis.*

3. Weimer and Vining, *Policy Analysis,* p. 61.

4. See Edith Stokey and Richard Zeckhauser, *A Primer for Policy Analysis* (New York: Norton, 1978), chap. 14; Weimer and Vining, *Policy Analysis,* chap. 5; Wolkoff, "Economic Development Financing Policy."

5. Richard Musgrave, *The Theory of Public Finance* (New York: McGraw-Hill, 1959).

6. See, for example, the argument in Peterson, *City Limits.*

7. Santa Barbara instituted a virtual moratorium on commercial development in 1987. Only projects already in the city's complex approval pipeline were allowed to go forward. The city is tying (or linking) the opportunity to enter the marketplace (that is, to develop) to the achievement of a specific city goal (such as the provision of low-cost visitor accommodations) and the local coastal plan. Commercial development is also linked to the housing supply. The city charges commercial developers a displacement fee—approximately $40,000—for each housing unit displaced. The city uses the fees to build housing in another location. A formula for residential construction, based on water supply, limits the

approval of new housing units to approximately 80 annually. Applicants for construction permits compete in a lottery for water rights.

8. George F. Lord and Albert C. Price, "Growth Ideology in a Period of Decline: Deindustrialization and Restructuring, Flint Style," *Social Problems* 39, no. 2 (1992): 155–69. The authors argue that AutoWorld's bankruptcy, within two years of its opening in 1986, "threatened to also bankrupt the city of Flint" (p. 159).

9. Wolf, "Market and Non-Market Failures."

10. For a detailed discussion of these and other forms of government failure, see Weimer and Vining, *Policy Analysis,* pp. 94–123.

11. See, e.g., Apogee Research, *Financing Infrastructure: Innovations at the Local Level* (Washington, D.C.: National League of Cities, 1987).

12. For an analysis of imputed costs, see Patrick Larkey, *Evaluating Public Programs* (Princeton: Princeton University Press, 1979).

13. Weimer and Vining, *Policy Analysis,* p. 116.

14. Louise Marshall, "New Evidence on Fiscal Illusion: The 1986 Tax 'Windfalls,'" *American Economic Review* 81, no. 5 (1991): 1336–44; Robert R. Logan and J. Patrick O'Brien, "Fiscal Illusion, Budget Maximizers, and Dynamic Equilibrium," *Public Choice* 63 (1989): 221–35; John G. Cullis and Philip R. Jones, "Fiscal Illusion and 'Excessive' Budgets: Some Indirect Evidence," *Public Finance Quarterly* 15, no. 2 (1987): 219–28; Daniel Hewitt, "Fiscal Illusions from Grants and the Level of State and Federal Expenditures," *National Tax Journal* 39, no. 4 (1986): 471–83; and David Lowery, "Opinion, Fiscal Illusion, and Tax Revolution: The Political Demise of the Property Tax," *Public Budgeting & Finance* 5, no. 3 (1985): 76–88.

Fiscal illusion is similar to the government failure identified by Weimer and Vining as "problems inherent in decentralization." A decentralized political system, such as American federalism, they argue, complicates "the implementation process" (*Policy Analysis,* p. 122) because of the difficulty in assessing the consequences of alternative policies, an argument we find contrary not only to Tiebout's argument concerning mobile citizens but also to the generally well-known economic and political benefits of decentralized federalist systems.

15. Ted Kolderie, "Changing Conceptions of the Governmental Role: Their Meaning for Urban Policy," in Charles Warren, ed., *Urban Policy in a Changing Federal System* (Washington, D.C.: National Academy Press, 1985), p. 264.

16. Aidan R. Vining and David L. Weimer, "Government Supply and Government Production Failure: A Framework Based on Contestability," *Journal of Public Policy* 10, no. 1 (1990): 1–22, 5, 8.

17. These collaborative public-private ventures can be either deal-specific or more broadly institutionalized. See the discussion in Max O. Stephenson, "Whither the Public-Private Partnership: A Critical Overview," *Urban Affairs Quarterly* 27 (Sept. 1991): 109–27.

18. David R. Morgan and William J. Pammer Jr., "Coping with Fiscal Stress: Predicting the Use of Financial Management Practices Among U.S. Cities," *Urban Affairs Quarterly* 24, no. 1 (1988): 69–86, 79.

19. For fiscal policy options during 1988–90, see Douglas D. Peterson, *City*

Fiscal Conditions in 1990 (Washington, D.C.: National League of Cities, 1990), p. 14; for 1991 data, see Michael A. Pagano, *City Fiscal Conditions in 1991* (Washington, D.C.: National League of Cities, 1991), p. 24.

20. Susan E. Clarke and Gary L. Gaile, "The Next Wave: Postfederal Local Economic Development Strategies," *Economic Development Quarterly* 6, no. 2 (1992): 187–98, 191, 192.

21. The City Market project also included two ancillary projects: a new public library and a small transit center. The Urban Mass Transportation Administration granted the city $181,718 for the transit center. The library was built with voter-approved general obligation bonds of $4,335,000 and private contributions of $1,400,000. These projects are excluded from the remaining discussion because they can be physically separated from the City Market project and because their success or failure only marginally affects the viability of the City Market and hotel project.

22. The tax-equivalency fund functions much like a tax-increment fund in that payments into the fund are used in the core redevelopment area only for development and commercial use (like parking). Credit Life Insurance Co. (CLICO) pays an in-lieu-of property tax fee to the fund because it also leases land from the city.

23. This figure is the estimated cost of the building and excludes machinery, furniture, inventory, and other costs.

24. The terms *present value subsidy* and *value-creating* are borrowed from Lynne B. Sagalyn, "Explaining the Improbable: Local Redevelopment in the Wake of Federal Cutbacks," *Journal of the American Planning Association* 56, no. 4 (1990): 429–41.

25. We devised a three-point scale for measuring the complexity of a project. A score of 1 signifies minimal oversight or policy development, a 2 means a mid-range of oversight, and a 3 means fairly constant oversight or considerable start-up administrative costs. The assignment of values is based on data collected from project files. A project received a 1 if it involved routine decisions, i.e., if city incentives were granted automatically. This included projects with a low level of staff involvement, low level of (or no) oversight costs, and minimal city council discussion. A project coded 3 required sustained city involvement, as indicated by repeated council deliberation, high oversight costs, or extensive preproject planning. The value 2 was assigned to projects falling between these endpoints. For this presentation, projects coded 1 and 2 were collapsed and labeled *routine,* projects coded 3 were labeled *complex.*

26. Lowell Historic Preservation Commission, "Preservation Plan," Sept. 4, 1980, p. 26.

27. Each UDAG repayment agreement designates a portion of the proceeds to be deposited in each of three accounts: industrial, commercial, and neighborhood/residential. The $5-million UDAG loan agreement to Wang Laboratories in 1978 required that 80 percent of the repayment funds be deposited in the industrial account, 10 percent in the commercial account, and 10 percent in the residential account. LDFC must secure the city council's approval of projects funded from the industrial account but not from the other two. The Hilton UDAG loan agreement and the Wannalancit loan (discussed below) required only 50 percent

of the repayment to be allocated to the industrial account and 50 percent to the residential or neighborhood account, reflecting a policy shift toward neighborhood development.

28. Robert R. Weaver, "Organizing and Staffing Local Economic Development Programs," in R. Scott Fosler, ed., *Local Economic Development* (Washington, D.C.: International City Management Association, 1991), pp. 101–9.

29. Dennis Judd and Michael Parkinson, "Urban Leadership and Regeneration," in Judd and Parkinson, *Leadership and Urban Regeneration,* p. 15.

30. For a discussion of the level of citizen involvement in the economic development process, see Sharp, "Institutional Manifestations."

CHAPTER 5 / MEASURING
SUCCESSFUL DEVELOPMENT

1. Efficiency and optimality tend to be peripheral to the decision to mobilize public capital. Witness the comments of the mayor of Providence, Rhode Island, Vincent Cianci, upon the opening of a new $356-million convention center complex in his city in 1993. "None of these things ever pay for themselves." Quoted in John Strahinich, "Mega-doubts," *Boston Globe,* Jan. 23, 1994.

2. Linder and Peters, "Instruments of Government," p. 37.

3. Ibid., p. 36.

4. Politicians as a group responded more positively to the How successful . . . question than city staffers did. Fortunately, we anticipated distorted or biased perceptions (i.e., responses that seemed at odds with empirical data), so we built some redundancy into our interviews by using multiple sources, follow-up interviews, and archival data.

5. Admittedly, one official might tell us X while a counterpart would tell us not-X. But by the time we had interviewed a series of officials and had examined relevant project information, we had a good indication whether X or not-X was accurate.

6. For a discussion of the concept of financial commitment, see Michael A. Pagano, "Urban Infrastructure and City Budgeting: Elements of a National Urban Policy," in Marshall Kaplan and Franklin James, eds., *The Future of National Urban Policy* (Durham: Duke University Press, 1990).

7. It is inappropriate to apply linear regression techniques to dichotomous dependent variables. Probit and logit are two statistical alternatives. We chose to use probit for our dichotomous dependent variables; logit results would have been virtually identical. See John H. Aldrich and Forrest D. Nelson, *Linear Probability, Logit, and Probit Models* (Beverly Hills, Calif.: Sage, 1984). Probit is especially useful with nonintervally measured dependent variables, such as the dichotomous yes or no answers and revenue generation variables.

Probit does not allow for the usual ordinary least squares interpretations of slopes or standardized betas; however, it does provide "the best, weighted linear combination of the independent variables." See John Aldrich and Charles F. Cnudde, "Probing the Bounds of Conventional Wisdom: A Comparison of Regression, Probit, and Discriminant Analysis," *American Journal of Political Science* 19 (Aug. 1975): 571–608, 581. For other uses and explanations of probit, see Timothy Bledsoe and Susan Welch, "The Effect of Political Structures on the Socioeconomic Characteristics of Urban City Council Members," *American Politics Quarterly* 13, no. 4 (1985): 467–83; and R. Douglas Arnold, *Congress and the Bureaucracy* (New Haven: Yale University Press, 1979).

The coefficients are not interpretable the way they are for linear regression. They can, however, be converted to probabilities. Before beginning the probit procedure, one adjustment was made to the data base. Factor analysis, using oblique rotation, identified that all variables save two were not correlated; only the visibility and complexity variables loaded on the same factor. Therefore, we removed the visibility variable from the analysis. This adjustment produced a six-variable model (two measures of resource intensiveness, one political risk variable, two constraint variables, and one financial risk variable). Three of the forty projects were in their early stages at the time of the fieldwork; thus success and revenue generation could not be measured for them, and they were removed from the analysis.

8. A pseudo R-square was calculated as, R-square $= c/(N + c)$, where $c =$ the chi-square statistic and $N =$ total sample size. See Aldrich and Nelson, *Linear Probability,* p. 57.

9. For an extensive discussion of this factor see Michael Pagano and Ann O'M. Bowman, "Risk Assumption and Aversion: City Government Investment in Development," paper prepared for the Annual Meeting of the American Political Science Association, Atlanta, 1989.

10. Lynn Bachelor concludes, from an analysis of Detroit's generous incentive packages for General Motors and Chrysler, that economic development decision-making is rarely rational. Informational asymmetries, time constraints uncertainty regarding the consequences of alternatives, and the importance of politics "preclude reliance on rational decision making." See Lynn W. Bachelor, "Regime Maintenance, Solution Sets, and Urban Economic Development," *Urban Affairs Quarterly* 29 (June 1994): 596–616, 613.

CHAPTER 6 / URBAN OUTCOMES

1. City officials are encouraged by economic development consultants to make their vision a consensus vision, that is, one shared by the community. See, for example, Hyett-Palma, "Retooling Your Local Economy," a workbook distributed at National League of Cities' economic development seminars in 1992. To achieve consensus, officials are urged to identify key stake holders and engage in a consensus-building process. Huntsville's Vision 2000 is an example of this approach.

2. John M. Findlay, *Magic Lands: Western Cityscapes and American Culture after 1940* (Berkeley: University of California Press, 1992), p. 3.

3. See the fascinating account of the St. Louis Arch (the Jefferson National

Expansion Memorial) in W. Arthur Mehrhoff, "The Image of the City: The Jefferson National Expansion Memorial as Monument to Progress," *Urban Affairs Quarterly* 24, no. 1 (1988):46–68. The underlying intentions and myriad consequences of such use of public capital are examined in Thomas H. O'Connor, *Building a New Boston: Politics and Urban Renewal, 1950–1970* (Boston: Northeastern University Press, 1993); and Joel Schwartz, *The New York Approach: Robert Moses, Urban Liberals, and Redevelopment of the Inner City* (Columbus: Ohio State University Press, 1993).

4. Findlay, *Magic Lands.*

5. Garreau, *Edge City*, Chap. 7.

6. Zukin, *Landscapes of Power.*

7. Susan Clarke notes that city officials make these decisions under conditions of limited information, external pressure, and fragmented local power structures. See Susan E. Clarke, "More Autonomous Policy Orientations," in Clarence N. Stone and Heywood T. Sanders, eds., *The Politics of Urban Development* (Lawrence: University Press of Kansas, 1987).

8. Charles C. Euchner, *Playing the Field: Why Sports Teams Move and Cities Fight to Keep Them* (Baltimore: Johns Hopkins Press, 1993), pp. 65–77.

9. A survey of 325 mayors shows that the primary goals of their economic development programs were increased employment and an improved tax base. See Ann O'M. Bowman, *The Visible Hand* (Washington, D.C.: National League of Cities, 1987).

10. See Stephen L. Elkin, *City and Regime in the American Republic* (Chicago: University of Chicago Press, 1987), chap. 3. Susan Clarke also argues that development policy is pursued in part as a response to electoral needs, thus improving the elected official's reelection prospects. See Clarke, "More Autonomous Policy Orientations."

11. Marc V. Levine, "Downtown Redevelopment as an Urban Growth Strategy: A Critical Appraisal of the Baltimore Renaissance," *Journal of Urban Affairs* 9, no. 2 (1987): 103–23.

12. J. Parton, "Pittsburgh," in Roy Lubove, ed., *Pittsburgh* (New York: New Viewpoints, 1976), p. 10.

13. In *Landscapes of Power,* Zukin argues convincingly that landscapes reflect a society's underlying social structure and power. Landscapes change as a consequence of creative destruction, in which a new configuration of power and authority replaces or modifies an earlier form.

14. O'Connor, *Building a New Boston,* p. 290.

15. J. W. R. Whitehead, *The Making of the Urban Landscape* (Oxford, Eng.: Basil Blackwell, 1992).

16. Frieden and Sagalyn, *Downtown, Inc.,* p. 15.

17. G. J. Ashworth and H. Voogd, *Selling the City: Marketing Approaches in Public Sector Urban Planning* (London: Belhaven, 1990), p. 3.

18. Scott Cummings, "Private Enterprise and Public Policy: Business Hegemony in the Metropolis," in Scott Cummings, ed., *Business Elites and Urban Development* (Albany: State University of New York Press, 1988).

19. O'Connor, *Building a New Boston,* p. xiii.

20. Glenn Collins, "Planner's Vision of Hall for Arts on the Passaic," *New York Times,* Apr. 6, 1993.

21. See, for example, Stone, *Regime Politics.*

22. What happens when the grand plans of city builders encounter the resistance of neighborhood groups is the subject of much analysis. One particularly compelling book is Chester Hartman's account of the Yerba Buena Center project in downtown San Francisco. See Chester Hartman, *The Transformation of San Francisco* (Totowa, N.J.: Rowman and Allanheld, 1984).

23. The economic fortunes of the high-technology industrial sector and, hence, of the city (and its government-supported projects) have been slipping since 1986. As late as 1989, Lowell hoped that the state's budgetary situation might change and that the University of Lowell would be new tenants of Wannalancit Mills.

24. Gregory Huskisson, "Indian-Run Gambling Casinos Worth a Look, City Official Says," *Detroit Free Press,* Jan. 30, 1992.

25. American Institute of Architects, Idaho Chapter, *Boise R/UDAT* (Boise: 1985), p. 11.

26. Milos Bobic, *The Role of Time Function in City Spatial Structures* (Aldershot, Engl.: Avebury, 1990), p. 232.

27. Fox Butterfield, "In New England, Worst Recession in U.S. Takes Hold," *New York Times,* July 23, 1990.

28. Garreau, *Edge City.*

CHAPTER 7 / ON POLITICS, MARKETS, AND IMAGES

1. Steven P. Erie, "Los Angeles Past Imperfect," *Urban Affairs Quarterly* 29 (Sept. 1993): 177–83, 179.

2. Zukin, *Landscapes of Power.*

3. HUD no longer calculates impaction and distress rankings, because the UDAG program no longer exists. Nevertheless, the quality points can be tabulated using HUD's formula. To have been eligible for UDAGs, one quality point was assigned for each of the eligibility criteria (namely, pre-1940 housing, per capita income change, poverty level, population growth lag, labor surplus area, job growth lag, and unemployment). A quality point was assigned when a city's statistics on these criteria were less than the median for all large cities except for the labor surplus area, which was based on the national average unemployment rate for two years. The hypothetical quality points identified in this discussion are estimates only and not taken from HUD. A calculation of quality points would have shown little change for several of the study cities between 1984–86 (the approximate years for which the 1987 UDAG index was created) and 1990–92 (the date of the decennial census and later observations about a city's activism). Santa Barbara, Huntsville, Orlando, Independence, and Boise would have remained in the low-distress category. On the "high-distress side, Springfield, with 7 quality points in the 1987 index, would have scored the same in 1990. Beaumont

had 5 quality points in 1987; in 1990 it would have had approximately 6. Evansville, with 4 in 1987, would have approximately 7, as would Duluth (5 in 1987). Lowell, a city classified as low distress in 1987, with 4 quality points, would have moved to the high-distress category in 1990, with nearly 7 quality points.

4. Butterfield, "In New England.

5. "In 1988 Wang had sales of $3 billion and employed more than 31,000 workers. Wang . . . now employs 6,000." See "Wang Headquarters Auctioned for $525,000," *New York Times,* Feb. 17, 1994.

6. In 1994, according to an official in Lowell's Planning and Development Department, Lowell had considerable unutilized factory and office space, and the recently elected city council would "really focus on economic development in order to fill up the empty spaces," especially recruiting small high-technology firms from around the region.

7. Wendy Warren, "Leaders Say Midlands Had to Fly with Air South or Lose Ground," *The State,* Feb. 20, 1994.

APPENDIX B / THE SUPPLY OF
DEVELOPMENT TOOLS

1. Advisory Commission on Intergovernmental Relations, *State and Local Roles in the Federal System* (Washington, D.C.: ACIR, 1982).

INDEX

Activism criterion, and selection of cities
for study, 5
Agglomeration economies, 30
Agricultural subsidies, 68
Akron, Ohio, 109
Alexandria, Va., 5
Amarillo, Tex., 5
Annexation of adjoining territory, 71–72
by Huntsville, 153–54
Army Ballistic Missile Agency, in Hunts-
ville, 9
Arvada, Colo., 5
Ashworth, G. J., 109
Aspirations, 27, 44
change in, 28
city squares as representing, 124
and economic changes, 140
economic development goals as, 24
and riskiness of development tools, 87
study question on, 7
and systems of cities, 28, 33–34
See also Perceptual orbits; Vision of
future cityscape
Assistance, as development tool, 84, 85
Athletics. See Sports
Atlanta, Georgia, xii, 109, 110

Baltimore, Md., 1, 45, 47, 64
Basic trading areas, 31–32
Bazaar, city as, 45
Beaumont, Texas, 5, 13–14
and analysis of development project
success, 93
development outcomes in, 131–33, 135
development tools of, 147–48
image of, 52, 61–63, 67
land area of (1940–1990), 146
as market city, 139
population of, 14, 144–45
and 10-percent contribution limit, 100
uncertain orbit of, 41
vision of, 52, 62–63
Beneficiaries of development project,
study questions on, 8
Berry, Brian, 31
Bloomington, Ind., 5
Boise, Idaho, 5, 16–17

and analysis of development project
success, 93
development outcomes in, 116–18, 121–
24, 135
development tools of, 138, 148–50
image of, 51, 52–53
land area of (1940–1990), 146
leadership change in, 52–53, 138
as maintenance/expansionist city, 139
orbit of, 38–39, 142
population of, 17, 144–45
and public-private partnership, 90
territorial accretion of, 71–72
vision of, 51, 53
Boston, Mass., 1, 63, 109–10
Boulding, Kenneth, 45
Bowman, Ann O'M., 4
Braun, Wernher von, 9
Brown, Rosellen, 45
Buffalo, N.Y., 1
Burnham, Daniel, 48
Business elite, 3

Canton, Ohio, 5
Capital investment and property values,
as development outcome, 107–8
in Boise, 116–18, 135
in Duluth, 111–13, 135
in Lowell, 113–15, 135
in Springfield, 115–16, 135
Casino gambling
cities defined by, 47
Duluth's investment in, 118–20
CDBG. See Community development
block grant program
Cedar Rapids, Iowa, 5
Central (downtown) business district
Boise's development of, 121–24, 149, 150
Duluth's development of, 111–13, 118–20
Evansville's development of, 126–28
Lowell's development of, 83, 129–31,
135, 156
Santa Barbara's revitalization of, 159
Springfield's development of, 66, 79,
116, 160 (see also City Market pro-
ject, Springfield)
vs. urban villages, 23

Central-place theory, 29–33
  modifications of, 33
  vs. perceptual orbits, 37
Charlotte, N.C., 49
Chattanooga, Tenn., 47
Chicago, Ill., 1, 31, 47, 109
Christaller, Walter, 29–30, 31
Cincinnati, Ohio, 65
Cisneros, Henry, 49
Cities
  causes of growth of, 1
  and changing environments, 2
  competition among, 2, 25, 34, 71, 140,
    141–42
  and development organizations, 87–88
  as dynamic and emerging, xii, 20, 137,
    138
  equilibrium sought by, 26
  in federal system, 25, 33, 34–37
  images of, 44–48, 51–52, 67 (see also
    Image)
  limits of influence of, 142
  Mumford on, 44
  provision vs. production of services by,
    74–75
  systems of, 22–24, 26, 33–37 (see also
    Systems of cities)
Cities, types of
  expansionist, 8, 27, 138, 139
  maintenance, 8, 27, 39, 124, 138, 139
  market, 8, 27, 139
  survivalist, 8, 27, 139
Cities in study, 9–19. See also Study on
  city development projects
City annexation of adjoining territory,
  71–72, 153–54
City Market project, Springfield, 78–82,
  103–4, 115–16, 135
City officials
  aspirations of, 24, 27, 44 (see also
    Aspirations)
  and market failure, 69
  perceptual orbits of, 37–43, 140–41,
    142 (see also Perceptual orbits)
  restraint of in exercising authority, 25
  selection of tools and techniques by,
    21, 23, 95
  and success measurement, 94–95
  and systems of cities, 22–24, 26, 28,
    33–34 (see also Systems of cities)
Cityscape
  and development projects, 20–21
  and politics-economics interaction, 137
  as text, 109
  vision of, xii, 2, 3, 20, 137 (see also
    Vision of future cityscape)

Clarke, Susan, 77
Classification of city, 8
  expansionist, 8, 27, 138, 139
  maintenance, 8, 27, 39, 124, 138, 139
  market, 8, 27, 139
  survivalist, 8, 27, 139
Class of user, as development outcome,
  109–11
  in Beaumont, 131–33, 135
  in Evansville, 126–28, 135
  in Lowell, 129–31, 135
  in Santa Barbara, 133–34, 135
Clearwater, Fla., 5
Cleveland, Ohio, 24
Columbia, S.C., 47–48
Columbus, Ohio, 48
Commission for a National Agenda for
  the Eighties, 35
Community development block grant
  program (CDBG), 35
  for Beaumont, 148
  in Boise, 150
  for Duluth, 151
  for Evansville, 126
  for Independence, 125, 155
  for Lowell, 156
  for Santa Barbara, 134
  for Springfield City Market project, 79,
    80, 81
Competition among cities, 2, 25, 34
  and airline example, 141–42
  and development investment, 71
  Duluth denies, 63
  and Lowell, 140
Complex development incentive packages, 84, 86–87, 172 n.25
Complexity of project, 96, 99, 102–3
Constraint, 96, 97
Corporate headquarters, in Boise, 16
Corporations, and perceptual orbits, 37–
  38
Costliness, project, 96, 99, 102
"Creative destruction," 138
Cyert, Richard, 26

Daily urban systems, 31
Dearborn, Mich., 5
Decatur, Ill., 5
Deconcentration, and Independence, 40
Defense-related (military) industry
  in Huntsville, 9
  spin-off industries from (Evansville), 13
Demand-side policies, 165 n.8
Density, questions on, 8
Denver, Colo., xi, 138
Detroit, Mich., 46, 168 n.11

Development, economic. *See* Economic development, public
Development mix, questions on, 8
Development outcomes, xiii, 106–7
  and capital investment and property values, 107–8, 111; Boise, 116–18, 135; Duluth, 111–13, 135; Lowell, 113–15, 135; Springfield, 115–16, 135
  and class of user, 109–11; Beaumont, 131–33, 135; Evansville, 126–28, 135; Lowell, 129–31, 135; Santa Barbara, 133–34, 135
  and intents, 134–36
  study question on, 7
  and vista or physical appearance, 108–9; Boise, 121–24, 135; Duluth, 118–20, 135; Independence, 124–26, 135; Lowell, 120–21, 131, 135
Development projects (programs), xi, 137, 142
  case studies on: Lowell Eastern Canal Park, 82–84; Springfield City Market, 78–82 (see also *other cities*)
  and efficiency, 75, 104
  entrepreneurial approach in, 77–78, 158
  image-creation value of, 24
  and politics, 21 (see also Politics)
  purposes in, 92, 106, 134
  selection of, 95
  study on, 4–19 (see also Study on city development projects)
  success of, 2–3, 92–95, 97–104 (see also Success of development projects)
  tax-services equilibrium over job generation as rationale for, 25–26
  tentative lessons from, 140–42
  for transportation infrastructure, 1–2
  and vision, 2
Development tools, 84, 91
  characteristics of, as determining success, 96–104
  financial component in, 84–87
  organizational component in, 87–90; in Huntsville, 153; Lowell Plan, Inc., 39, 55–56, 88–90, 129
  selection of, 21, 23, 25
  supply-side and demand-side, 165 n.8
  used by study cities: Beaumont, 147–48; Boise, 138, 148–50; Duluth, 150–51; Evansville, 152–53; Huntsville, 153–54; Independence, 154–55; Lowell, 156–57; Orlando, 157–158; Santa Barbara, 158–59; Springfield, 160–61
  See also Public capital mobilization
Dillon, John F., 36

Direct investment, 84, 85. *See also* Investment
Disneyland, 106
Disney World, 11, 57, 109
Distress criteria, UDAG, 4–5, 98–99, 176 n.3
Diversification of economic base
  by Duluth, 63
  by Lowell, 55–56
Diversifinancing, 147–48
Downtown. *See* Central business district
Duluth, Minn., 5, 12
  and analysis of development project success, 93
  development outcomes in, 111–13, 118–20, 135
  development tools of, 150–51
  image of, 52, 63–64
  land area of (1940–1990), 146
  population of, 12, 144–45
  as survivalist city, 139
  uncertain orbit of, 41–42
  vision of, 52, 63–64
Durham, N.C., 5

Eastern Canal Park (Jack Kerouac Commemorative Park), Lowell, 82–84, 93, 94, 101, 120–21
East St. Louis, Ill., 10
Economic development, public, xiii
  and image, 48–49, 67
  1980s assumption of, 49
  and political decisions, 2–3
  questioning of, 49
  reasons for, 3–4
  See also Development
Economic development administration programs, 35
Economic health of cities
  and project success, 98–99, 101–2, 104, 137, 141
  and riskiness of development tools, 87, 88
Economic restructuring, and central-place theory, 31
Efficiency, economic
  and government failure, 73, 75
  and government intervention, 69, 70, 72, 104
  and market failure, 68, 69–70
  and market price on government services, 77
  and project success, 28, 92
  in public investment, 95
Eminent domain, and Lowell, 82, 156–57
Enterprise zones, 37

Enterprise zones (*con't.*)
 in Evansville, 152
 and Independence, 155
 in Springfield, 160
 in Texas, 147
Entertainment industry, and Orlando
 area, 11, 40
Entrepreneurial approach
 for development programs, 77–78
 by Orlando, 158
Erie, Steven, 138
Erie Canal, and Buffalo, 1
Evansville, Ind., 5, 12–13
 and analysis of development project
 success, 93
 development outcomes in, 126–28, 135
 development tools of, 152–53
 image of, 52, 64–66
 land area of (1940–1990), 146
 population of, 13, 65, 144–45
 and public-private partnership, 90
 as survivalist city, 139
 uncertain orbit of, 41–42
 vision of, 52
Expanding orbits, 38–40
Expansionist cities, 8, 27, 139
 Boise as, 138
Externalities. *See* Spillovers

Failure. *See* Government failure; Govern-
 ment market failure; Market failure
Failure, chance of (project characteristic),
 97
Federal spending, in Huntsville, 54
Federal system, cities in, 33, 34–37
 and exercise of full city authority, 25
Fee-based pricing structure, 77, 78
Financial component, of development
 tools, 84–87
Financial risk, 88, 96, 97, 99, 100, 102
Findlay, John, 106
Fiscal externalities, 73–74
Fiscal illusion, 74, 171 n.14
Flint, Mich., 72
Flynn, Patricia, 56
Fond-du-Luth Casino, Duluth, 93, 118–
 20, 135
Frieden, Bernard, 109

Gaile, Gary, 77
Garcia v. San Antonio Metropolitan
 Transit Authority, 35
Garreau, Joel, 23
Gary, Ind., 10
Gentrification, 110
Glendale, Calif., 5

Golden Triangle, 41, 61
Gottdiener, M., 50–51
Government failure, 72–75, 91
 and riskiness of development tools, 87
Government market failure, 76–78
 and city as investor (Lowell), 82–84
 and city as subsidizer (Springfield), 78–
 82
Green Bay, Wis., 5
Growth of cities, economic causes of, 1
 and Kansas City vs. Independence, 17
 second-generation (Santa Barbara), 18

Hampton, Va., 5
Heritage State Park, Lowell, 82–84, 120
Hierarchy of cities, in central-place the-
 ory, 29. *See also* Systems of cities
High-tech images, for Huntsville, 54
High-technology corridor, Atlanta-to-
 Memphis, 39, 54
High-technology industry
 and Boise, 149
 in Lowell, 56, 129
 in Santa Barbara, 18
Home rule, 36–37
Housing density bonus program, in
 Orlando, 101, 103
Houston, Tex., 28, 45, 47, 107
Howard, Ebenezer, 48
HUD loan guarantees, for Beaumont, 148
HUD UDAG program. *See* Urban development action grant program
Huntsville, Ala., 5, 9–10
 and analysis of development project
 success, 93
 in competition with Lowell, 34
 development authority in, 90
 development tools of, 153–54
 as expansionist city, 139
 image of, 51, 53–55, 67
 land area of (1940–1990), 146
 orbit of, 39, 142
 population of, 9–10, 144–45
 vision of, 51, 54

Ideology, urban image as, 50
Image(s), 44–48, 67
 change in, 50, 138
 creation of, 50–51
 around Duluth casino, 120
 and economic development, 24, 48–49,
 67
 influences on, 139
 as political foundation, 142
 power of, xii
 and purpose of city investment, 141

of study cities, 51–52; Beaumont, 52, 61–63, 67; Boise, 51, 52–53; Duluth, 52, 63–64; Evansville, 52, 64–66; Huntsville, 51, 53–55, 67; Independence, 52, 58–60; Lowell, 52, 55–57, 67; Orlando, 52, 57–58, 67; Santa Barbara, 52, 60–61; Springfield, 52, 66–67
Incentives, development, 84, 91
 purpose of, 106
 in Springfield retention of International Harvester, 161
 tax, 147 (*see also* Property tax abatement)
 See also Development tools
Independence, Mo., 17
 and analysis of development project success, 93
 development outcomes in, 124–26, 135
 development tools of, 154–55
 image of, 52, 58–60
 joint venture in, 90
 land area of (1940–1990), 146
 as maintenance city, 139
 and political risks, 100–101
 population of, 17, 59, 144–45
 self-contained orbit of, 40–41
 and trading areas, 32
 vision of, 52
Industrial revenue bonds, for Duluth, 151
Industry. *See* High-technology industry; Manufacturing; Oil industry
Informational asymmetries, 70, 74
Infrastructure, local
 Duluth's providing of, 151
 Evansville's renovating of, 65
 as Huntsville tool, 55, 153–54
 as Independence tool, 154–55
 on Orlando agenda, 11
 state investment in, 37
 and Tax Reform Act, 35
Inglewood, Calif., 5
In-lieu-of payment, for Springfield, 80, 81, 160–61
Internationalization, economic, and regionalism, 23
Internationalization of capital, and spatial dominance of market areas, 34
Interstate highway system, 34
 and Huntsville, 55, 154
Intrusiveness, project, 97, 99, 102
Investment, xiii
 and development project success, 28
 direct, 84, 85
 by Lowell (Kerouac Park), 82–84
 rationale for, 95

return on, as benchmark, 93
 in Springfield central business district, 66
 study question on, 7
 See also Capital investment and property values
Investment scandal, in Beaumont, 62

Job generation, and development-project rationale, 25–26
Judd, Dennis, 90
Jungle, city as, 45

Kansas City, Mo., 17
Kerouac, Jack, 82
Kerouac Commemorative Park (Eastern Canal Park), Lowell, 82–84, 93, 94, 101, 120–21
Kolderie, Ted, 74
Kucinich, Dennis, 24

La Colina housing project, Santa Barbara, 93, 133–34, 135
Lafayette, La., 6
Lakewood, Colo., 6
Land use
 as Boise tool, 149
 and Evansville development, 126
 questions on, 8
Langdon, Philip, 23
Lansing, Mich., 5
Le Corbusier, 48
Linder, Stephen, 95
Little Rock, Ark., 6
Loan programs, Beaumont's use of, 147–48
Local leaders. *See* City officials
Los Angeles, Calif., 46, 138
Lowell, Mass., 5, 10–11, 139–40
 and analysis of development project success, 93
 and Beaumont, 41
 in competition with Huntsville, 34
 development outcomes in, 113–15, 129–31, 135; Eastern Canal Park (Jack Kerouac Commemorative Park), 82–84, 93, 101, 120–21; Hilton Hotel, 93, 129–31, 135; Wannalancit Office and Technology Center, 93, 113–15, 135
 development tools of, 156–57
 expanding orbit of, 39–40
 image of, 52, 55–57, 67
 investment by (Eastern Canal Park), 82–84
 land area of (1940–1990), 146

Lowell, Mass., (con't.)
  as maintaining boundaries, 72
  physical appearance as outcome for, 109
  popular and political support for proj-
    ect in, 100
  population of, 10, 144–45
  public-private organization (Lowell
    Plan, Inc.), 39, 55–56, 88–90, 129
  as survivalist/expansionist city, 139
  and trading areas, 32
  vision of, 52, 56, 131, 139–40
Lowell Development and Financial Corporation (LDFC), 89–90
Lynch, Kevin, 46

Machine, city as, 45
Maintenance cities, 8, 27, 139
  Boise as, 39, 138
  Independence as, 124
"Major league," 49
Mall
  Boise's development of, 116–17
  competition for Lowell from, 140
  competition for Springfield from, 66
  planned near Manassas, Va., 135–36
Mandates, federal, 35–36
Manhattan skyline, 46
Manufacturing
  defense-related, 9, 13
  and Duluth, 12
  and Evansville, 13
  locational characteristics for, 15
  and Springfield, 15
  textile (Lowell), 10, 55, 56
March, James, 26
Market areas, 34
Market cities, 8, 27, 139
Market failure, xiii, 68, 91
  and area of control, 142
  and city situations, 70–72
  government, 76–84
  and government behavior, 104
  and success of development project,
    28, 92–93
  types of, 69–70
Market forces
  and position in system of cities, 23
  and urban development patterns, 20
Market signals, reliance on, 97, 99, 102
Marshall Space Flight Center, Huntsville, 9
Meaning, and image, 50
Mental maps, of local political elites, 51
Miami, Fla., 46
Miami Beach, Fla., 5
Military industry. See Defense-related
  industry

Minneapolis, Minn., 42
Mobilization of public capital. See Public
  capital mobilization
Monopolies
  governments as, 73
  natural, 69
Monterey, Calif., 47
Mumford, Lewis, 44
Musgrave, Richard, 70

National Road, and Springfield, 15–16
Nesting, in urban systems, 31
Newark, N.J., 10, 110
New Orleans, La., 47
New York City
  buildings symbolizing, 47
  and central-place hierarchy, 31
Niche-seeking, xii, 3. See also Perceptual
  orbits
1982 National Urban Policy Report, 35
No-risk development tools, 84, 85

Ohio River, and Evansville, 12–13
Oil industry, in Beaumont, 14
Orbits. See Perceptual orbits
Organism, city as, 45
Organizational component of development tools, 87–90
  in Huntsville, 153
  Lowell Plan, Inc., 39, 55–56, 88–90,
    129
Orlando, Fla., 5, 11–12
  affordable housing program in, 101,
    103
  and analysis of development project
    success, 93
  aspirations of, 140
  development authority in, 90
  development tools of, 157–58
  as expansionist city, 139
  image of, 52, 57–58, 67
  land area of (1940–1990), 146
  orbit of, 38, 40, 142
  population of, 11, 144–45
  territorial accretion of, 71–72
  vision of, 52
  and Walt Disney World, 11, 57, 109
Outcomes. See Development
  outcomes
Oxnard, Calif., 5

Parking facilities
  for Lowell, 129, 156
  for Santa Barbara, 159
Parkinson, Michael, 90
Peoria, Ill., 5

Perceptions
  and political behavior, 33–34
  of project success, 95
Perceptual orbits, xii, 37–38, 43, 140–41
  expanding, 38–40
  influences on, 139
  as political foundation, 142
  self-contained, 38, 40–41
  uncertain, 38, 41–43
Perry, George, 45
Peters, Guy, 95
Peterson, Paul, 2, 25, 49
Physical appearance, as development outcome, 108–9
  in Boise, 121–24, 135
  in Duluth, 118–20, 135
  in Independence, 124–26, 135
  in Lowell, 120–21, 131, 135
Pittsburgh, Pa., 1, 42, 65, 109
Political behavior, perceptions of, 33–34
Political risk, 96–97, 98–99, 102, 104–5, 141
Politics
  and city-sponsored projects, 21
  importance of, xi–xii, 2–3
  and perceptual orbits, 43, 142
  and systems of cities, 22, 33–37
  and urban development patterns, 20
Population growth
  and Evansville, 65
  and Independence, 59
  1900–1990 table on, 144–45
  of Orlando, 11
  and Santa Barbara policy, 18
Portsmouth, Va., 5
Pricing strategies, marketlike, 77
Primate city, 29
Private capital investment, and cityscapes, 20–21
Production of benefit, vs. provision, 74–75
Project outcomes. *See* Development outcomes
Property tax abatement
  in Beaumont, 147
  and capital investment, 108
  in Evansville, 152
  in Springfield, 160
Property values, as development outcome, 107–8
  in Boise, 116–18, 135
  in Duluth, 111–13, 135
  in Lowell, 113–15, 135
  in Springfield, 115–16, 135
Proposition 2½, Massachusetts, 76
Proposition 13, California, 76, 77

Providence, R.I., 5
Provision of benefit, vs. production, 74–75
Public capital, 21
Public capital mobilization, xi, xii, 20, 21–22, 137–38
  and change in economic foundations, 140
  changes in, 138
  as purposive, 106
  and system of cities, 22–24, 26
  and tax-services equilibrium, 22, 24–27
  trigger mechanisms for, 26–28
  See also Development tools; Economic development, public
Public goods, 69
Public investment. *See* Investment
Public sector
  and Huntsville, 54
  marginalization of, in literature, 137

Rabe, Barry, 25
Raleigh, N.C., 6
Rand McNally, trading areas defined by, 31–32
Reading, Pa., 5
Redevelopment, 109–10
Redstone Arsenal, 9
Reductionism, in understanding of cities, 46
Regulatory action, federal, 35
Rent seekers, and government failure, 72–73
Research Triangle, 40, 140
Resource balance, for Santa Barbara, 60, 61
Resource intensiveness, 96
Revenue generation, and policy characteristics, 101–4
Richardson, Harry, 29
Risk
  financial, 88, 96, 97, 99, 100, 102
  political, 96–97, 98–99, 102, 104–5, 141
  for routine vs. complex packages, 86–87
Routine development incentive packages, 84, 86–87, 172 n.25

Sagalyn, Lynne, 109
St. Louis, Mo., 47, 109
San Antonio, Tex., 49
San Jose, Calif., 47
Santa Barbara, Calif., 5, 18–19
  and analysis of development project success, 93
  aspirations of, 140

Santa Barbara, Calif., (con't.)
  development outcomes in (La Colina housing), 133–34, 135
  development tools of, 158–59
  image of, 52, 60–61
  improvement-management in, 103
  land area of (1940–1990), 146
  land demand in, 71
  as maintenance city, 139
  population of, 18, 144–45
  and public-private partnership, 90
  self-contained orbit of, 41
  vision of, 52, 60–61
Santa Monica, Calif., 6
Savannah, Ga., 5
Schneider, Mark, 24
Seattle, Wash., 47, 107
Second-generation growth management, and Santa Barbara, 18
Self-contained orbits, 38, 40–41
Semiotics, 50
Services and taxes. See Tax-services equilibrium
Service sector, and central-place theory, 31
Shannon, James, 39, 88
Silicon Valley, 40, 63, 107, 140
Site visits, for study of cities, 6–8
Skyline, city, and development-project study, 8
Small-business incubators, 37
Social organizations, environmental adaptation of, 26
South Bend, Ind., 5
South Carolina v. Baker, 35
Spatial considerations
  central-place theory, 29–33
  and evaluation of project success, 93, 95
  and fiscal externalities, 74
  and government-intervention rationale, xiii, 68–69, 71, 91
  and government production, 75
  and market areas, 34
Spillovers (externalities), 70
  in Boise mall development, 118
  fiscal, 73–74
  study questions on, 8
  and study selections, 6
Sports
  Charlotte NFL stadium, 49
  1991 World Series, 46
  Orlando NBA team, 58
  and San Antonio's major-league dome, 49
  stadium construction, 108
Springfield, Mo., 5
Springfield, Ohio, 5, 15–16

  and analysis of development project success, 94
  City Market project of, 78–82, 103–4; as development outcome, 115–16, 135
  development tools in, 160–61
  image of, 52, 66–67
  land area of (1940–1990), 146
  as market city, 139
  orbit of, 42–43, 142
  population of, 15, 144–45
  vision of, 52, 66–67
Stamford, Conn., 6
State governments, cities' relations with, 36
Steel industry, and Duluth, 12
Stone, Clarence, 3
Study on city development projects, xii, 4
  cities in, 9–19, 138–39 (see also particular cities)
  on efficacy of development projects, 141
  generalizability of, 141
  previsit contacts for, 6
  and project success, 95–104
  and routine vs. complex development packages, 84, 86–87, 172 n.25
  selection of cities for, 4–6
  site visits for, 6–8
Subsidies, xiii
  agricultural, 68
  and development project success, 28
  indirect, 84, 85
  by Springfield (City Market), 78–82
  study question on, 7
Success of development projects
  definition and measurement of, xiii, 2–3, 28, 92–95
  and development tools, 96
  and economic health, 98–99, 101–2, 104, 137, 141
  perception of, 95–96
  as problematic, 92
  study findings on, 97–104
  study questions on, 7
Sunnyvale, Calif., 5
Supply-side policies, 165 n.8
Supreme Court, on federal role, 35
Surrogate property tax (in-lieu-of payment), Springfield, 80, 81, 161
Survivalist cities, 8, 27, 139
Suttles, Gerald, 51
Systems of cities
  and central-place theory, 29–33
  evolution of, 28
  and leaders' perceptions, 33–34
  and politics, 33–37

and public capital mobilization, 22–24, 26

Tax abatement, 85. *See also* Property tax abatement
Tax-equivalency fund
of Springfield, 80, 81, 160, 172 n.22
See also Tax-increment financing
Taxes
from Boise development, 118
from Duluth central business district, 113
and government failure, 76–77
as revenue source, 78
Tax incentives
Beaumont's use of, 147
See also Property tax abatement
Tax-increment financing (TIF), 151
for Boise, 123, 149
for Duluth, 111, 150–51
and Independence, 125–26, 155
for Orlando, 157
for Santa Barbara, 103, 133–34, 159
See also Tax-equivalency fund
Taxpayer revolts, 76
Tax Reform Act (1986), 35, 149
Tax-services equilibrium, 22, 24–26
and economic development, 140–41
influences on, 139
and public intervention, 69, 95
and search for development policy, 26–27
Tempe, Ariz., 6
Texas Energy Museum, Beaumont, 93, 131–33, 135
Textile industry, in Lowell, 10, 55, 56
Thünen, Heinrich von, 30
TIF. *See* Tax-increment financing
Toledo, Ohio, 64
Topeka, Kans., 6
Tourism
in Beaumont, 132
in Duluth, 63, 120
in Independence, 59, 125
in Lowell, 129, 156
in Orlando area, 11
in Santa Barbara, 18
Towne Square Mall, Boise, 93, 116–18, 135
Transportation costs
and central-place theory, 29
and market areas, 34
and system of cities, 22, 23
von Thünen's study of, 30
Transportation infrastructure
city and state investment in, 1–2

and Huntsville, 55, 154
and Orlando, 11
Truman, Harry, and Independence, 58, 59, 124
Tsongas, Paul, 39, 88
Tully, B. Joseph, 39, 88
Tyler, Tex., 6

UDAG. *See* Urban development action grant program
Uncertain orbits, 38, 41–43
Unemployment
and development projects, 26
as distress criterion, 5
Unfunded mandates, 35–36
Urban centers, in central-place theory, 29
Urban development action grant (UDAG) program, 35
in Boise, 150
for Duluth, 151
for Lowell, 89, 113–14, 129–30, 156
for Springfield, 79, 80, 81, 103
Urban development action grant (UDAG) rating system for distressed cities, 4–5, 98–99, 176 n.3
Urban development intervention, xii. *See also* Public capital mobilization
Urban economic development policy, 20, 21
Urban economic development projects. *See* Development projects
Urban-hierarchy analysis, 33. *See also* Central-place theory
Urban renewal programs, 109–10
in Boise, 121, 149–50
Urban villages, 23
of Orlando, 57
User, class of. *See* Class of user
User fees, 77, 78

Vallejo, Calif., 5
Vining, Aidan, 72, 74
Visibility, of project, 96–97
Vision of future cityscape, xi, xii, 2, 3, 20, 137
evolution of, 23, 50, 138
and outcomes, 107
problematic attainment of, 92
and project success, 94
and riskiness of development tools, 87
of study cities: Beaumont, 52, 62–63; Boise, 51, 53; Duluth, 52, 63–64; Evansville, 52; Huntsville, 51, 54; Independence, 52; Lowell, 52, 56, 131, 139–40; Orlando, 52; Santa

Vision of future cityscape (*con't.*)
  Barbara, 52, 60–61; Springfield, 52, 66–67
  study question on, 7
Vista. *See* Physical appearance
Voogd, A., 109

Wabash-Erie Canal, 13
Walnut Centre, Evansville, 93, 126–28, 135
Walt Disney World, 11, 57, 109
Wannalancit Office and Technology Center, Lowell, 93, 113–15, 135

Washington, D.C., 47
Weimer, David, 72, 74
Weirton, W.Va., 107
Winston-Salem, N.C., 5
Wolf, Charles, 72
Wolman, Harold, 21, 51
Wong, Kenneth, 25
"World class," 49, 169 n.25
World War II, and Lowell decline, 10

Zoning changes, 110

Library of Congress Cataloging-in-Publication Data

Pagano, Michael A.
  Cityscapes and capital : the politics of urban development / Michael
A. Pagano and Ann O'M. Bowman.
    p.   cm.
  Includes bibliographical references and index.
  ISBN 0-8018-5034-7 (alk. paper)
    1. Urban renewal—United States—Case studies.   2. Urban policy—
United States—Case studies.   3. Metropolitan government—United
States—Case studies.   4. Municipal government—United States—Case
studies.   5. Urban economics—Case studies.   I. Bowman, Ann O'M.,
1948– . II. Title.
HT175.P32   1995
307.3'416—dc20   94-40582

ISBN 0-8018-5767-8 (pbk.)